Care of Churches
and Ecclesiastical
Jurisdiction Measure
CODE OF PRACTICE

CHURCH HOUSE PUBLISHING
Church House, Great Smith Street, London SW1P 3NZ

ISBN 0 7151 3753 0

Published 1993 for the General Synod of the Church of England by Church House Publishing

© *Central Board of Finance of the Church of England 1993*

The drawing on the front cover is of All Saints Church, Hutton, Essex, and is reproduced by kind permission of the Rector.

Printed in England by Rapier Press Ltd

CONTENTS

3

FOREWORD

The Measure for which this is the Code of Practice is a major part of an agreement reached between the General Synod and the Department of the Environment concerning the proper protection of churches which are listed buildings. It deals also with the Church's own concern for the right ordering of places of worship. The right observance of this agreement is not only a matter of the integrity of the Church in its undertakings but also directly related to the continuance of the Ecclesiastical Exemption.

Legal documents almost inevitably seem complex at first sight, but I hope it will be realised that to a very considerable extent this one simply reflects existing best practice. I commend the Code to all who have to deal with this area of the Church's life believing that it is for the common good.

+Eric Cicestr:

I INTRODUCTION

The New Legislation

1   When the Care of Churches and Ecclesiastical Jurisdiction Measure 1991 (referred to throughout this Code as 'the 1991 Measure') comes into force on 1st March 1993, the Measure and the Rules made under it will have a major impact on the law and practice affecting the Church of England's churches, their contents and the churchyards and other land which belong to them. All those who are concerned with the care or conservation of these parts of the nation's and the Church's heritage will need to familiarise themselves with the new law and be ready to apply it, and this Code is intended as a practical guide to help them in doing so.

2   The legislation stemmed from recommendations by the Faculty Jurisdiction Commission, under the chairmanship of the Bishop of Chichester, whose report *The Continuing Care of Churches and Cathedrals* was published in 1984. In addition to the 1991 Measure, the legislation consists at present of the Faculty Jurisdiction Rules 1992 (referred to in this Code as 'the Faculty Jurisdiction Rules') and the Faculty Jurisdiction (Injunctions and Restoration Orders) Rules 1992 (referred to as 'the Enforcement Rules'). Other Rules on miscellaneous matters will follow.

General Principles

3   The 1991 Measure aims to ensure that churches and everything which belongs to them are properly cared for, and that whatever is done to them is properly considered beforehand and carried out in the best possible way. However, churches are not only historic monuments; they exist for a purpose – the worship of God and the mission of His Church – and they have a vital role to play in the life of the Church, both now and in the future. They should be living buildings, which fulfil and are seen to fulfil that role. Thus the 1991 Measure begins by providing that:

> Any person or body carrying out functions of care and conservation under this Measure or under any other enactment or rule of law relating to churches shall have regard to the role of the church as a local centre of worship and mission (s.1).

5

4   These principles are, of course, the ones which both clergy and lay people within the Church of England are already applying in practice. They are proud of the fact that churches and their contents are among this country's finest historic, artistic and architectural treasures. Churches are also important from an archaeological point of view, and churchyards in particular are often sanctuaries for wildlife which is disappearing elsewhere. It has been and will continue to be the Church's task to safeguard this inheritance, which has been handed down by past generations of Christians and which is part of the life of the whole community.

5   The 1991 Measure, with its new legal framework, is a further step in securing that the twin aims of safeguarding the inheritance of the past, and fulfilling the local church's living role as a centre of worship and mission, are not incompatible. The keys to reconciling them lie in ensuring that the parish:

(a)   takes expert advice at an early stage about any project affecting the church, its contents or its churchyard or other land, and consults all those who have a legitimate interest in the project, both inside and outside the Church, before finalising the proposals and taking a definite decision to seek approval for them; and

(b)   complies scrupulously with the Church's own legal requirements and any other legislation affecting the project.

6   Taking these steps will avoid wasted time, energy and money, and is vital in order to obtain financial assistance for the project from 'official' sources (particularly English Heritage) where that is available. Moreover, the fact that the Church has its own comprehensive system of legal controls means that it is exempt from some aspects of the normal (secular) legislation affecting buildings of historic or architectural interest, conservation areas and ancient monuments. This leaves it with greater flexibility to use its buildings so as to meet the needs of the living Church, while at the same time giving due weight to all the various 'heritage' considerations. It is essential that everyone with a role to play in the care and conservation of churches and all that belongs to them should understand and observe both the letter and the spirit of the new legislation, so that the Church's special position in this respect is seen to work well in the interests of the whole community and can be preserved for future generations.

How to Use this Code

7   A wide variety of people will be involved under the new legislation, and all of them will find useful information in this Code. However, it is not intended as a detailed legal text-book – some of these are listed in Appendix H – or as a substitute for reading the text of the 1991 Measure and the Rules themselves. It is essentially a practical guide, which summarises the main provisions of the 1991 Measure and the Rules and contains recommendations as to good practice, many of them taken

from the Faculty Jurisdiction Commission's report, and it is intended to meet the needs of three categories of people in particular:

(a) *those concerned with the care and conservation of churches in the parish.* They will be provided by dioceses with basic guidance on the new legislation, in leaflet or similar form. This Code supplements that guidance, by providing a more comprehensive reference document with detailed information on particular topics; it also gives a broad picture for the non-specialist of the Church's legal arrangements for these matters and the way in which they are expected to work in practice;

(b) *archdeacons,* whose long-standing role in relation to the care of churches has been greatly extended by the 1991 Measure and the Rules made under it. This Code aims to provide them with practical advice in exercising their new powers and fulfilling their new responsibilities; and

(c) *members and secretaries of Diocesan Advisory Committees,* which again have an enhanced role and functions under the 1991 Measure and Rules, as well as a new constitutional framework. They too need practical guidance in implementing the new legislation.

8   To guide each of these categories of people in their particular needs, the following is a brief guide to the various Sections and Appendices of this Code:

Section II, on people, bodies and organisations, gives a broad overview of the Church of England's legal arrangements for the care and conservation of its churches and what belongs to them. All those who use this Code are encouraged to read it at the outset.

Section III, on the continuing tasks of care and conservation, is of particular concern to parishes. Ministers and churchwardens should read the whole of it as soon as possible, and then turn to it later for reference when necessary. The same applies to archdeacons, who will need to supervise parishes in fulfilling their obligations as well as exercising some new powers of their own, and to rural deans. The material on inspection of churches, the contents of churches and churchyards will also be of particular concern to Diocesan Advisory Committees.

Section IV, on Diocesan Advisory Committees, will principally be of interest to members and secretaries of those Committees, including archdeacons, who are members by virtue of their office. However, it will also be helpful for others, particularly in parishes, to read through the Section and gain a general idea of what the Diocesan Advisory Committee is, how it functions and how it can help them. For this reason, some of the more detailed material has been separated from the main text and placed in Appendix A. When a parish reaches the stage of applying for a faculty, it will need to refer again to this Section.

Sections V and VI are intended mainly for parishes and archdeacons, and deal firstly with the preliminary steps towards repairs, alterations and additions to churches, their contents and churchyards, and then with the faculty jurisdiction, which controls work of this kind. Those involved in parishes should, at least, read the two sections and study the flow chart in Appendix B if and when a proposal for repairs, alterations or additions comes up for consideration. Archdeacons, who will need to deal with such cases on a routine rather than a 'one off' basis, are recommended to read through the whole of the two Sections. Individual paragraphs will be of particular concern to Diocesan Advisory Committees, but they will also find it helpful to have a broad idea of the contents of both Sections at the outset. Appendices C, D, E and F are also linked to Section VI.

Sections VII and VIII are mainly intended for reference so far as parishes and Diocesan Advisory Committees are concerned, but parts of them deal with new powers given to archdeacons, so that archdeacons are recommended to gain a general idea of their contents at an early stage. Appendices G and H also contain reference material, but those who have a particular interest in the subject may like to follow up some of the suggestions for further reading in Appendix H even if they are not confronted immediately with any specific problems under the new legislation.

9   This Code is a working document. It has been produced so that it can easily be converted into a loose-leaf form, for insertion into a ring-binder bought from any stationer. One reason for this is to help users keep all the relevant material, including diocesan leaflets and the like, together and ready for immediate use. In addition, it is intended that supplements will be issued from time to time to bring the contents up to date and to deal with points thrown up by practical experience of the working of the 1991 Measure and the Rules. All those who buy this Code are therefore asked to return the form enclosed with it to the General Synod Office, so that they can receive information about the supplements as and when these are issued. In addition, suggestions for amendments or new material will be gratefully received, and should be sent to the Assistant Legal Adviser, General Synod Office, Church House, Great Smith Street, London SW1P 3NZ.

II PEOPLE, BODIES AND ORGANISATIONS –
AN OVERVIEW OF THE SYSTEM

Introduction

10   This section gives a brief account of the main people, bodies and organisations which have a role to play under the 1991 Measure and the Rules. In doing so, it provides a general overview of the Church's legal system for the care and conservation of churches, their contents and churchyards, and shows how the 1991 Measure and Rules are built on the structure which was already in place before they were passed. However, the list of those involved in this aspect of the Church's work is not an exhaustive one; in particular, a number of other specialised bodies will be mentioned in Sections III, V and VI.

11   In this Section and those which follow, reference to specific provisions of the 1991 Measure and the Rules appear in the column on the right hand of the page. Except where stated otherwise, the references are to the Measure; 'FJR' indicates a reference to the Faculty Jurisdiction Rules and 'ER' to the Enforcement Rules. Other legal references are given in notes at the end of each Section.

The Parish

12   The parish is at the heart of the organisation of the Church of England, and it is also at the heart of most of the Church's arrangement for caring for and preserving churches and all that belong to them. The 1991 Measure and the Rules apply to all parishes in England, and the term 'parish' in the legislation also includes areas which are formally constituted as conventional districts. The legislation does not apply automatically to the Isle of Man and the Channel Isles, but it may be extended to them in the future with whatever modifications are needed to take account of their own special legal systems.

s.31(1)
s.33(3)

13   The main people and bodies involved at parish level under
the 1991 Measure and the Rules are:

(a)   *the minister* (usually the rector, vicar or team rector or,   s.31(1)
if there is none, the priest in charge. In the case of a team
ministry, a team vicar who has a 'special cure of souls' in
respect of the parish will be the minister under the 1991
Measure);

(b)   *the churchwardens*; and

(c)   *the parochial church council.*

14   All of these already have important functions in relation to
the church, its contents and the churchyard. The minister usually
has control over the church and churchyard and in many cases he
will also hold the legal title to the property for the use and benefit
of the parishioners. The churchwardens have legal ownership and
custody of the moveable goods belonging to the church, again for
the use and benefit of the parishioners. Even before the 1991
Measure the Church's Canon law also required the minister and
churchwardens to keep a terrier and inventory of the land and
property of churches and required a record to be kept of all alterations, additions, removals or repairs to the fabric, ornaments or
furniture.[1] The parochial church council is responsible, among other
things, for the financial affairs of the parish; for the care, maintenance, preservation and insurance of the fabric of the church and its
goods and ornaments; and for the care and maintenance of the
churchyard[2] unless, in the case of a closed churchyard, that responsibility has been transferred to the local authority (see para. 77).[3]
The council is also encouraged to appoint a fabric officer to assist
the minister and churchwardens with their duties in relation to the
fabric and contents of the church.

15   The 1991 Measure has developed this system. In particular,
the churchwardens' duties to record information about churches are   s.4
strengthened, and they are also required to make at least annual   s.5
inspections of the fabric of the church and the articles belonging to
it and to make annual reports to the parochial church council and to
the annual parochial church meeting of those on the church electoral
roll. These duties, which are to be carried out in consultation with
the minister, are described in more detail in Section III (see paras
46-60), as are the revised provisions for professional inspection of   Sch.3
and reports on churches at least every five years (see paras 29-45).[4]

16   In cases where a district church council and, possibly, deputy

churchwardens have been formally appointed for a church or place of worship (other than the parish church) which lies within the parish,[5] the parochial church council and the churchwardens may be able to delegate some or all of their functions in relation to that church or place of worship to the district church council and deputy wardens. The parish should consult the diocesan registrar about the extent to which this is legally possible in any particular case.

The Diocese and the Archdeaconry

17   At the diocesan level, the following all have new functions under the 1991 Measure:

(a)   *the bishop*. He is the chief minister of his diocese, who is ultimately responsible for the supervision and pastoral care of the Church and of everyone and everything which belongs to it within the diocese. Together with the powers and duties which he already had, the 1991 Measure gives him important new powers and duties in relation to the care and conservation of churches, including the making of a number of key appointments (in some cases after consultation with others) (see, for example, sub-paras (d) and (e) of this paragraph and paras 96(a) and 104); a reserve duty to impose a diocesan scheme for the professional inspection of churches if the diocesan synod fails to provide one (see para.31); responsibility for directing who is to receive duplicate copies of inventories and how often they are to be updated (see para. 53); power to remove the legal effects of consecration from land or buildings in certain very limited circumstances (see paras 217-220), and power to exclude places of worship which have not been consecrated from the faculty jurisdiction or the system of professional inspection, after consultation with the Diocesan Advisory Committee (see paras 39 and 138(d)). In some cases, his functions may be delegated to an area or other suffragan bishop[6] or some other person in episcopal orders;[7]

Sch.3 para.3

s.4(4)

s.22

s.11(3)
Sch.3 para.5

(b)   *the bishop's council*, which is also the *standing committee of the diocesan synod.*[8] Under the 1991 Measure it is responsible for appointing most of the members of the Diocesan Advisory Committee (see para. 96(c)) and it is consulted about the appointment of the chairman (see para.96(a)). It will also wish to keep under review the way in which the arrangements for the care and conservation of churches and all that belongs to them – and especially the new legislation – are working in practice in the diocese, so

Sch.1 para.4

Sch.1 para.3

that any problems can be raised at an early stage in the diocesan synod or taken up with whoever is directly responsible for the particular matter;

(c) *the Diocesan Advisory Committee* (referred to in this Code as 'the DAC'). This Committee has had advisory functions for many years. Because of the major impact the 1991 Measure had on it it is dealt with separately in Section IV;

(d) *the chancellor* (in the diocese of Canterbury known as the commissary general). He or she is an experienced barrister or (under the 1991 Measure) solicitor, or a person who has held office as a senior judge in the secular courts, and must be either a member of the clergy or a lay person who is a communicant member of the Church of England.[9] The chancellor is appointed by the bishop, after consultation with the Lord Chancellor and with the Dean of the Arches and Auditor (an ecclesiastical judge of the Province), to be the judge of the ecclesiastical court of the diocese, which is known as the consistory court (in Canterbury the commissary court).[10] Occasionally the consistory court hears disciplinary cases, but its main function is to deal with petitions for faculties (that is, permissions) to carry out repairs, alterations or additions to churches, their contents and their churchyards[11] and related matters. Under the 1991 Measure a clearly limited but substantial power to grant faculties will also be delegated to the archdeacon, and the archdeacon therefore forms part of the consistory court for that purpose (see para. 161). The faculty jurisdiction, and the chancellor's role under it and in other exceptional cases, including enforcement proceedings, are dealt with in more detail in Sections VI to VIII. The new requirement in the 1991 Measure for the bishop to consult the Lord Chancellor before appointing a person as chancellor emphasises the fact that the chancellor is one of Her Majesty's Judges, and not merely a diocesan official. In addition, the Faculty Jurisdiction Commission wished to encourage suitable new lawyers to enter the ranks of the chancellors, and recommended that those who wished to be considered for appointment to chancellorships should submit their names to the Dean of the Arches and Auditor, who must also be consulted on new appointments.[12] Further provisions of the 1991 Measure reduce the retiring age for chancellors and provide for the appointment of deputies;

Sch.4 para. 2(b)

Sch. 4 para. 2(a)

s.14

Sch.4 paras 2 & 4

12

(e) *the diocesan registrar* The registrar of the diocese is a solicitor who must be 'learned in the ecclesiastical laws and the laws of the realm' and who is a communicant member of the Church of England.[13] He or she is appointed by the bishop after consultation with the bishop's council,[14] and the 1991 Measure also provides for the appointment of a deputy registrar. The registrar has a wide range of legal responsibilities within the diocese. These include the duty to act as registrar, or clerk, to the consistory court;[15] as such, the registrar is responsible for ensuring that all petitions for faculties are properly dealt with and for keeping the records of the court, and the registrar's role in relation to faculty matters is described in more detail in Section VI. In addition, the registrar receives an annual retainer for giving advice to incumbents and other clergy, churchwardens and secretaries of parochial church councils (among others);[16] this duty, although subject to some qualifications, extends to all legal matters properly arising in connection with those people's duties, and they should not hesitate to approach the registrar at an early stage with any queries about the legal position, rather than running the risk of creating problems for the parish later.

Sch.5 para.3

18   *The archdeacon* has always had a vital part to play in the care and conservation of churches and all that belongs to them within the archdeaconry. However, that role has been greatly enhanced by the 1991 Measure and the Rules, so that archdeacons will need to be prepared for an increased workload and may well need additional resources, particularly in terms of secretarial help, in order to carry it out.

19   The following Sections of this Code give a detailed description of the archdeacon's new functions. However, a brief summary of some of the archdeacon's new and existing powers and duties in relation to churches, their contents and churchyards, is given here, in order to indicate the general nature of the archdeacon's role, to show how wide-ranging and vital it is, and to give an idea of how the different elements relate to one another. Broadly, the archdeacon's enlarged functions fall into three categories:

(a) *supervisory and enforcement* Under Canon law,[17] the archdeacon must assist the bishop in his pastoral care and office; must see that all who hold ecclesiastical office perform their duties with diligence; and must hold yearly visitations of parishes, survey all churches and churchyards in the archdeaconry every three years, and give directions for amending defects. In addition, the archdeacon has statutory enforcement of and other powers under the system of regular professional inspections of and reports on churches[18] (see para. 45), and power to order the removal of articles belonging to the church to a place of safety (see paras 66-70); these are explained more fully in Section III. Even before the 1991 Measure the archdeacon had certain powers to initiate or intervene in faculty proceedings and could be asked to supervise work authorised for a faculty.[19] These provisions reappear, sometimes in a slightly modified form, in the new legislation, but the 1991 Measure also makes provision for cases where the archdeacon is to carry out work authorised by a faculty if the parish fails to do so (see para. 186), and the Enforcement Rules add a new role in the new types of proceedings to enforce the faculty jurisdiction (see paras 225 and 227). The archdeacon also has a new power to convene an extraordinary parochial church council or parish church meeting to discuss any failure to fulfil the legal requirements at parish level (see paras 229-231). All these enforcement powers relating to the faculty jurisdiction are considered in more detail in Section VIII. Finally, it is the archdeacon who sets in motion the procedure for removing the legal effects of consecration from land or buildings in a restricted category of cases (see para. 218);

s.21

s.12(1)(a) & 16

s.12(2)

ER r.3

s.20

s.22

(b) *advisory* Quite apart from the archdeacon's general role in giving advice to parishes on a host of matters, including those in relation to churches, their contents and churchyards, all archdeacons are members of the DAC by virtue of their office (see para. 96(b)); and

Sch.1 para.2

(c) *judicial* As already indicated (see paras 17(d) and 161), the archdeacon will now have delegated authority from the chancellor to grant faculties, mainly in uncontroversial cases, and will form part of the consistory court for that purpose. The 1991 Measure and the Faculty Jurisdiction Rules lay down detailed rules as to the exercise of this new power, and further information is given about them in Section VI. In addition, the archdeacon has a limited power to authorise temporary re-ordering of churches without a faculty; this is explained in Section VII.

s.14

FJR r.8

20   Although the archdeacon's supervisory and enforcement powers and duties might seem to predominate in the previous paragraph, the 1991 Measure places them firmly in the context of a general role as a link between the parish and those involved in the

central administration of the diocese. Indeed, the Faculty Jurisdiction Commission saw the archdeacon as 'the anchorman of the whole system of communication between the parish and the diocese'.[20] It is essential that the parish sees the archdeacon as one of the first points of contact for guidance, particularly when there are proposals for repair, alterations or additions to the church, its contents or the churchyard (see para. 122(b)) and that the archdeacon encourages them to do so; this not only ensures the smooth running of the system of legal controls over the Church's buildings and their contents and land but also provides a major opening for the archdeacon's pastoral work with the parish.

21   The *rural dean* assists the archdeacon in various respects, for example in relation to surveys of churches.[21]

Other Local Bodies

22   The *local planning authority* may be involved in faculty proceedings, as well as in the exceptional procedure for demolition without a faculty (see paras 172, 178, 194(c) and 214). Works proposed by the parish may also require planning permission under the ordinary planning legislation, or listed building or conservation area consent, in addition to a faculty, and in that case the local planning authority will need to be approached for the necessary permission or consent (see para. 132(a)).

National Bodies

23   *The Council for the Care of Churches* not only co-ordinates the work of DACs but also interprets the activities of the Church concerning church buildings, furnishings, and other contents and churchyards to national heritage and amenity bodies (see, for example, paras 24 and 25). Besides its general advisory, conservation and publicity activities, the Council has specific duties under the faculty jurisdiction. The chancellor will give it an opportunity to advise in most cases of total or partial demolition (see para. 194(b)) and where a petition for a faculty concerns or involves an article of historic or artistic interest (see para. 173), and it has a right to apply to give evidence in any case. In addition, the chancellor will frequently consult the Council where a case involves technical matters or where a DAC is deeply divided in its opinion or has become heavily involved in the local issues. DACs will often anticipate such requests by asking for preliminary advice from the Council. However, the Council does not usually deal directly with a parish on faculty matters, except by agreement with the secretary of the DAC for the

s.17(4), 17(6)
FJR r.12,21
FJR r.14
FJR r.22(2)

15

diocese concerned. The bishop is also required to consult the Council before appointing the chairman of the DAC (see para. 96(a)).

Sch.1 para.3

24 *English Heritage* (formally known as the Historic Buildings and Monuments Commission for England) is statutory adviser to both the Secretary of State for the Environment and the Secretary of State for National Heritage on all aspects of conservation policy. English Heritage makes recommendations to the Secretary of State for National Heritage on the listing of buildings (both secular and ecclesiastical) and advises him, the Secretary of State for the Environment and local planning authorities on conservation policy and archaeology. English Heritage also advises the Secretary of State for the Environment and local planning authorities on many individual listed building consent applications, particularly those concerning Grade I and Grade II* buildings. In London, English Heritage has power to direct local planning authorities as to the manner in which they may decide listed building consent applications. English Heritage also administers funds provided by Government for the repair of historic buildings and has a general responsibility to promote the highest standards of conservation and preservation of historic buildings. For example, it has produced a Policy Statement on New Work in Historic Churches (see Appendix H) providing guidance on that subject. As regards its role under the 1991 Measure and the Faculty Jurisdiction Rules, in particular in relation to the faculty jurisdiction, and in consultation over the membership of the DAC, see paras 96(c), 135, 172, 174, 182 and 194(c).

25 *English Nature* (formally known as the Nature Conservancy Council for England) is the statutory adviser to Government on nature conservation in England and promotes the conservation of England's wildlife and natural features; its powers and duties include important statutory functions under the Wildlife and Countryside Act 1981, and it also has certain powers to make discretionary grants (see paras 81 and 127).

26 The statutory *National Amenity Societies* must by law be informed of any applications for listed building consent in England and in Wales involving any degree of demolition of a listed building. The Societies are also consulted on a regular basis by local planning authorities on applications for planning permission to extend listed churches. They are all 'National Amenity Societies' for the purpose of the 1991 Measure; as regards their role in faculty proceedings, see for example paras 172, 178 and 194(c). The Societies are:

s.31(1)

(a) The *Ancient Monuments Society*, which is concerned with historic buildings of all ages and all types but with a particular interest in churches through the formal association since 1980 with the Friends of Friendless Churches;

(b) The *Council for British Archaeology*, which is concerned with all historic buildings but with a particular interest in the archaeology of subterranean and standing structures;

(c) The *Society for the Protection of Ancient Buildings*, which is concerned mainly with structures constructed before 1700 but also with philosophical and technical aspects of conservation;

(d) The *Georgian Group*, which is concerned with architecture and architecture-related arts between 1700 and 1840; and

(e) The *Victorian Society*, which is concerned with Victorian and Edwardian architecture and architecture-related arts from 1840 to the First World War.

In addition, the *20th Century Society* (previously known as the Thirties Society) has been designated as one of the National Amenity Societies for the purpose of the 1991 Measure. It is concerned with architecture of the 20th Century in all decades except the first. Although it is not formally recognised as a full National Amenity Society under the secular planning legislation, it is recognised by Central Government as a relevant body to be approached by local planning authorities in dealing with post-1910 structures. s.31(1)

27   The addresses and telephone numbers of all these national bodies can be found in Appendix G.

Notes

1. Canons E 1, F 13 and F 17.

2. Parochial Church Councils (Powers) Measure 1956 s.4(1)(ii).

3. Local Government Act 1972 s.215.

4. Under the Inspection of Churches Measure 1955.

5. Church Representation Rules (Synodical Government Measure 1969 Sch.3) r.16; Pastoral Measure 1983 Sch.3 para. 4(2).

6. Dioceses Measure 1978 s.10 and 11.

7. Church of England (Miscellaneous Provisions) Measure 1983 s.8.

8. Church Representation Rules r.28(1).

9. Ecclesiastical Jurisdiction Measure 1963 s.2, as amended by the 1991 Measure.

10. Ecclesiastical Jurisdiction Measure 1963 s.1(1) and 2, as amended by the 1991 Measure.

11. Ecclesiastical Jurisdiction Measure 1963 s.6(1).

12. *The Continuing Care of Churches and Cathedrals*, para. 224.

13. Canon G 4.

14. Ecclesiastical Judges and Legal Officers Measure 1976 s.4(3).

15. Ecclesiastical Judges and Legal Officers Measure 1976 s.4(2)

16. Under Orders under s.5 of the Ecclesiastical Fees Measure1986

17. Canons C 22 and F 18.

18. Inspection of Churches Measure 1955 s.2.

19. Faculty Jurisdiction Measure 1964 s.9 and 10.

20. *The Continuing Care of Churches and Cathedrals*, para. 85.

21. Canons C 22 and F 18.

III CARE AND CONSERVATION
– THE CONTINUING TASKS

Introduction

28.   From the point of view of the parishes, sections 3 to 5 of the
1991 Measure, which fall within the part of the Measure headed
'Care, Inspection and Accountability', will be the most important
provisions on a 'day to day' and 'year by year' basis. They deal

primarily with the routine but essential tasks of recording information about the church and all that belongs to it, regular inspection and regular reports, all of which are vital elements in the care of the church, its contents and the churchyard. In addition, this Section of the Code deals with some specific topics relating to contents of churches, churchyards and ruins which have caused particular difficulty or are of particular importance in practice. To some extent the provisions of the Measure build on the existing law and the best existing practice, so that much of what they contain will not be wholly new to parochial clergy, churchwardens and parochial church councils. However, it is important that all concerned – those involved in the parish, the archdeacon and the members and secretary of the DAC – should familiarise themselves with the new requirements as soon as possible, and work out a forward plan for putting them into practice.

Professional Inspection and Reports on Churches – the Inspection of Churches Measure 1955

29   Since the Inspection of Churches Measure 1955 ('the 1955 Measure') came into force, the Church of England has had a country-wide system for the regular professional inspection of all churches and professional reports on them at least every five years, so that matters which need attention are highlighted and can be dealt with at as early a stage as possible. The 1991 Measure strengthens and extends that system, and (except where otherwise stated) the paragraphs which follow set out the position under the 1955 Measure in its amended form.

THE DIOCESAN SCHEME

30   Each diocese is required to establish a scheme to provide for the inspections and reports mentioned in the previous paragraph. The scheme must also establish a fund, to be raised from parochial, diocesan or other sources; the scheme will normally provide for the inspections to be paid for out of the fund, but the Measure does not rule out the possibility of meeting the cost in some other way. In addition, the scheme must provide for the inspections and reports to be made by architects or, under the 1991 Measure, chartered building surveyors who in either case are approved by the DAC, and must deal with the people and bodies to whom copies of the report are to be sent (see para. 43). The diocesan synod may also include its own provisions in the scheme, so long as these are not inconsistent with the statutory requirements.[1]

31   Even though more than thirty years have passed since the 1955 Measure came into operation, and its basic requirements as

regards inspections and reports are now an accepted part of the life of the Church, some diocesan synods have not yet adopted formal schemes. If they fail to do so once the 1991 Measure has come into force, the bishop will be under a duty to establish the scheme himself. Where a diocese does not already have a scheme, it is recommended that the DAC encourages the diocesan synod to adopt one as soon as possible and, if that fails, asks the bishop to take action. In either case, it may be helpful for the DAC, in consultation with the diocesan registrar, to prepare a draft scheme on the basis of the model in Appendix I to the Council for the Care of Churches publication *A Guide to Church Inspection and Repair* (see Appendix H). Sch.3 para.3

32   In addition, dioceses which already have formal schemes will normally need to revise them in line with the provisions in the 1991 Measure as to the people who may be appointed to carry out inspections and make reports, the scope of the inspections and reports and the people and bodies to whom the reports are to be sent. Here too, it is suggested that the DAC takes the lead, and prepares details of the amendments in consultation with the diocesan registrar.

THE INSPECTING ARCHITECT OR SURVEYOR

33   The inspection must be carried out, and the report made, by a qualified professional person approved by the DAC.[2] Under the original 1955 Measure that person had to be a qualified architect, but under the 1991 Measure it is also possible to appoint a chartered building surveyor who is a member of the Royal Institution of Chartered Surveyors. Sch.3 paras 2,4 & 5

34   Each DAC will already have its own system and criteria for approving architects and, broadly, these should also be followed for surveyors. However, it is recommended that all DACs review their own arrangements once the 1991 Measure comes into force, so as to take account of the new legal requirements (for example, as regards the scope of the inspection and report – see para. 41) and the best practice in the country as a whole. Among the points which it is recommended that the DAC should consider here are the following:

(a)   the need to approve individuals rather than firms, bearing in mind that personal qualifications, the personal link with the parish and personal responsibility for the work are all essential elements;

(b)   the importance of ensuring that those who are on the 'approved list' do not merely have appropriate 'paper qualifications' (essential though these are) but also have suitable practical experience. The approved architect or surveyor needs to be a person who is expert and experienced in the care and conservation of historic buildings, and who is properly sensitive to the historic, architectural and liturgical context of churches. To help ensure this, DACs are advised to require all applicants to complete a pro forma giving details of their experience as well as their professional qualifications. So far as chartered building surveyors are concerned, the Royal Institution of Chartered Surveyors has run its own conservation course for some years, and also has an accreditation scheme for its members so far as work on historic buildings is concerned. If DAC secretaries are in doubt they should contact the Institution's head office (see Appendix G). It is also recommended that DACs try to ensure those on their 'approved lists' devote a substantial proportion of their continued professional development to subjects which are relevant to work on ecclesiastical buildings or historic buildings generally. Membership of learned societies, such as the Association for Studies in the Conservation of Historic Buildings, the Ecclesiastical Architects and Surveyors Association and the Society for the Protection of Ancient Buildings (see Appendix G), is also something to be encouraged;

(c)   the need to encourage younger architects and surveyors into the field, perhaps by allowing their appointment at first to less demanding buildings or by encouraging them to work with senior colleagues, who are already on the 'approved list', on churches and comparable buildings, and monitoring their performance or arranging for their senior colleague to do so. Otherwise the younger professionals are caught in the vicious circle of not being admitted to the 'approved list' because they have no experience and yet being denied the chance of acquiring that experience; and

(d)   the fact that some categorisation of churches may also be helpful to parishes in choosing an appropriate person, although it is also important to stress that there are no 'second class churches' and that modern buildings may present major problems as difficult as any encountered in older ones.

35   It is also important for the DAC to maintain regular contact with the people whom it has approved to carry out inspections, and to encourage the less experienced to develop their skills. One useful way of doing this is to hold regular seminars or conferences on at least an annual or biennial basis, possibly with a paper or talk on a

topic of particular interest, but also with ample time for the architects and surveyors to raise questions about matters which they have encountered in practice and to pass information to each other and to members of the DAC.

36   Although inspecting architects and surveyors have to be approved by the DAC, they are appointed by the individual parishes. If a parish is approached by or is already in contact with a suitably qualified person whom it wishes to consider for appointment but who is not already on the 'approved list', it can encourage the person concerned to apply to the DAC for approval and, where appropriate, to support the application.

37   Once the inspecting architect or surveyor has been appointed, it is also most important that the parish and the architect or surveyor should build up and maintain a close relationship, quite apart from the five-yearly inspections. Church architects and surveyors play a key role in the life and development of the parish and its church. The longer they have a church in their care, the greater their specialised knowledge of the particular building and its problems. It makes sense if the person who carried out the inspection is also retained to deal with any subsequent repairs and alterations. Thus the same degree of skill and expertise can be brought to bear in advising parishes on the preparation of faculty applications (see paras 122(c) and 130), in helping to draw up clear and concise details of the work (see para. 141), in obtaining quotations and prices, and in inspecting the progress of the work to its completion. Not only does this enable the parish to foster a closer relationship with its professional adviser, but it will also help to ensure that the parish's funds and other resources are used wisely and effectively. In cases where the parish considers it can undertake the work satisfactorily on its own, the DAC will normally wish to know that the church's inspecting architect or surveyor has been consulted about the proposals and considers that they are satisfactory and make sense in an overall strategy of care and conservation.

THE INSPECTION AND REPORT

38   The 1955 Measure in its original form was limited to consecrated churches and chapels.[3] However, the 1991 Measure extends it to a wider category of buildings – in addition to all *parish churches* (including any that have previously regarded themselves as 'peculiars' and exempt from the normal requirements) and all other *consecrated churches and chapels* (other than cathedrals and churches or chapels which are not subject to the jurisdiction of the

Sch.3 para. 5(a)

diocesan bishop), it also includes all *buildings licensed for public worship*, subject to very limited exceptions. This is a major change in the 1955 Measure, bearing in mind the increasing numbers of new places of worship which are not being consecrated but merely licensed in order to preserve maximum flexibility for the future.

39 There are three exceptions to the general rule that licensed buildings are now within the scope of the 1955 Measure. Two of them relate to buildings which are in universities, colleges, schools or hospitals or other public or charitable institutions (such as prisons and almshouses), and buildings used solely for religious services relating to burial and cremation (such as chapels at cemeteries and crematoria). The third exception is that the bishop may direct, with the approval of the DAC, that a particular building should be excluded. However, it is recommended that this power is used only in exceptional cases, in view of the fact that modern buildings need regular maintenance and repair from the moment they are built, and that regular inspection is the best and most cost-effective way of achieving this.

Sch.3 para. 5(a)

40 The 1955 Measure does not apply to cathedrals other than parish church cathedrals which have 'opted' for the faculty jurisdiction under the Care of Cathedrals Measure 1990.[4]

41 In addition to the fabric of the church, the 1991 Measure also lays down three items which must be included in the inspection and report:

Sch.3 para.3

(a) *movable articles* in the church which the archdeacon, after consulting the DAC, directs the architect or surveyor carrying out the inspection to include, on the basis that they are of outstanding architectural, artistic, historical or archaeological value, or of significant monetary value, or at special risk of being stolen or damaged. Thus it is recognised that important or vulnerable contents call for regular expert inspection just as much as the fabric itself, and architects and surveyors carrying out inspections are also to take the initiative in including any movable articles which they consider fall within those headings even if the archdeacon has not directed them to do so. Examples might include, for example, tapestries and pictures, but the range of possible objects is extremely wide, and the contents of each church will need to be considered on an individual basis. However, some or all of the items in question, such as hatchments and paintings, may well call for specialist knowledge, and both archdeacons and those carrying out inspections need to be aware of the limitations of their own knowledge and expertise and be willing to call in outside help where needed. For example, there will probably be a local museum which can give advice, and if the DAC is not able to help the Council for the Care of Churches can give advice from its own resources or suggest possible experts. It is also important to take common sense security precautions in dealing with these important or vulnerable contents in the inspection report, which will normally have a fairly wide circulation. In particular, it is recommended that a confidential list of the articles covered is kept in secure conditions by the incumbent and churchwardens, the archdeacon and the DAC, but that the report does not list them, and does not refer to specific articles except so far as that is essential in order to make the recommendations intelligible;

(b) *ruins in churchyards* (whether open or closed – see para. 77) which the Council for British Archaeology ('the CBA') and the Royal Commission on the Historical Monuments of England ('the RCHME') have designated as of outstanding architectural, artistic, historical or archaeological value. This provision, and the provision explained in paragraph 91, follow a survey of ecclesiastical ruins which was carried out under the auspices of the CBA in the 1980s, and which is now available for most counties. If there is any doubt as to whether a particular ruin has been designated, the parish or person carrying out the inspection should consult the CBA or the RCHME direct (see Appendix G). 'Ruin' has a technical meaning in the 1991 Measure, and if questions arise as to whether a particular structure falls within it the diocesan registrar should be consulted; and

Sch.3 para. 5(b)

(c) *trees in churchyards* (whether open or closed – see para. 77) *which are subject to tree preservation orders.* These are part of the Church's heritage, in which the community has an interest in the same way as in the fabric of the church, and which should also be regularly inspected. It is also recommended that the inspection covers *all trees in any churchyard which is in a conservation area.* Here again, however, expert knowledge may well be needed; for this, the diocese may have one or more tree advisers who can assist, and it is recommended that DACs which have not already done so should draw up a list of suitably qualified profes-

25

sionals in the area. In addition, advice should be available from a tree specialist appointed by the local authority (see also para. 87).

42   It is recommended that the inspection and report follow the guidelines laid down in Appendices I and III of the Council for the Care of Churches booklet *A Guide to Church Inspection and Repair* (see Appendix H); this will ensure that the inspection itself is thorough and systematic, and will help to achieve a degree of uniformity in presentation. To assist the parish in making decisions as to the work to be carried out, it is recommended that reports should summarise the priority of any remedial work which is required, and indicate the urgency and time-scale of the work recommended. Items which can be dealt with by the parish on a do-it-yourself basis should also be identified. While general advice on the anticipated cost of the work is not strictly part of the inspection scheme, it will of course be useful to the parish.

43   Copies of the report must be sent to the incumbent, the parochial church council, the archdeacon and the DAC secretary. As a matter of good practice, it is also recommended that a copy should be sent to the rural dean.

Sch.3 para. 2(b)

44   The report will be a key document for action in preserving the fabric of the church and the other items covered, both on a short and a long term basis. However, it is important to remember that the report does not set out to provide a precise specification of any repairs or other work which it recommends, and that the specification will need to be drawn up separately. In addition, the fact that a particular item of work appears in the report does not remove the need for a faculty before it is carried out (see Section VI).

THE ARCHDEACON'S DEFAULT POWERS

45   If the archdeacon finds that a church, or any movable article which has been designated under the powers mentioned in paragraph 40(a), has not been satisfactorily inspected for at least five years, the archdeacon may require the parochial church council to arrange for an inspection. Where parishes fail to do this, archdeacons may, with the consent of the bishop, arrange for inspections themselves and recover the cost from the fund set up by the diocesan scheme.[5]

Duties of Churchwardens – Recording Information, Inspection and Reporting

46   The 1991 Measure, building on and strengthening existing Canon law provisions,[6] requires the churchwardens:

     (a) to compile and maintain a full *terrier* of all lands belonging to the church and a full *inventory* of all articles belonging to the church; and   s.4(1)(a)

     (b) to maintain a *log-book* containing a full note of all alterations, additions and repairs to the church and the land and other articles belonging to it, other events affecting any of them, and the location of any relevant documents which are not kept with the log-book itself.   s.4(1)(b)

This duty applies in relation to each church – defined as in paragraphs 38-40 – in the parish, and a separate terrier, inventory and log-book are needed for each one.   s.4(5)

47   The form of these documents is to comply with the recommendations made by the Council for the Care of Churches. The Council has recommended the use of the existing loose leaf forms of terrier and inventory and log-book published for the Council by Church House Publishing. These forms are available from Church House Bookshop, Great Smith Street, London SW1P 3BN, from the Council for the Care of Churches and from other booksellers, and contain detailed instructions as to how they should be completed. They are already in use in many parishes, but even where a terrier and inventory using the recommended forms are already in existence the churchwardens should check and update them once the 1991 Measure comes into force.   s.4(3)

48   As well as a written record of the articles belonging to the church, it is essential to keep an adequate photographic record, which would be particularly important if an article is stolen.

49   Compiling an inventory often calls for specialist knowledge. Churchwardens are encouraged to make use of the services of the National Association of Decorative and Fine Arts Societies ('NADFAS') (see Appendix G), which organises teams of volunteers to visit individual churches and compile full and systematic records of furnishings and other contents to a high standard. Such a record is a great help to the churchwardens in compiling the inventory, and should be kept with it. A copy of the NADFAS report is also deposited with the Council for the Care of Churches. In any

case, it is recommended that churchwardens whose churches own articles of any significant value or historic interest should seek advice from the DAC about compiling the inventory.

50   Occasionally questions of ownership may arise regarding articles or land which apparently belong to the church. In that event it is important to consult the diocesan registrar before any attempt is made to resolve the position.

51   If the church or anything on the land belonging to it is a listed building, it is recommended that a copy of the list description (produced by the Department of National Heritage and available from the local authority) is kept with the terrier.

52   In any event, it is vital that the terrier, inventory and log-book should be kept up to date on a regular and systematic basis. The same also applies to any NADFAS record or valuation.

53   As soon as practicable after the inventory has been compiled, the churchwardens must send a copy to the person designated by the bishop. They must also send details of any alterations to the same person at intervals fixed by the bishop. It is recommended that the bishop consults the DAC and the archdeacon before giving his directions. Who is the most suitable person to receive the documents (for example, the archdeacon, the secretary of the DAC or possibly in some cases the diocesan record office) will depend on which of them has a large amount of storage space available in conditions which are secure against fire, damp and theft, where the archdeacon has ready access to the documents and where they are available in an emergency, possibly out of normal office hours.   s.4(4)

54   The inventory should be kept in a secure place – generally in the church safe. In view of the growing number of thefts of church property, it is recommended that both the inventory and the copy are treated as confidential, and are made available only to those who can establish a legitimate reason for needing to see the document. If the copy inventories are deposited in the diocesan record office, they will therefore need to be subject to a special condition restricting public access to them.

55   It is also recommended that where the archdeacon needs copies of the log-book and other parish documents, photocopies are used as far as possible – the loose leaf form of the log-book should help considerably here – instead of copying out the information into other documents.

56   In compiling and maintaining the terrier and inventory and   s.4(2)
maintaining the log-book, the churchwardens must act in consultation with the minister. As soon as practicable in each calendar year   s.5(4)
they must also produce the terrier and inventory and the log-book   s.5(7)
covering the previous year to the parochial church council, together
with a signed statement that the contents are accurate and any other   s.5(5)
records which the churchwardens consider are likely to help the
parochial church council in discharging its functions as regards the
fabric of the church and the articles belonging to the church. It is
recommended that the parochial church council regards the inspection
of these documents as an important part of its duties in respect of the
care, maintenance and preservation of the fabric of the church and its
goods and ornaments and the care and maintenance of the churchyard (see para. 14), and does not merely take the item 'on the nod'.

INSPECTION AND REPORTING

57   The 1991 Measure also imposes two new legal requirements
on churchwardens, together with a third requirement which builds
on the existing provision in the Church Representation Rules for a
fabric report to be made to the annual parochial church meeting.[7]
However, many churchwardens will find that there is very little in
the new provisions which they have not already been doing for some
time as a matter of good practice.

58   The three requirements are:

(a)   to *inspect* the fabric of the church and all the articles   s.5(1)(a) & (7)
belonging to it at least once every calendar year;

(b)   to *make an annual fabric report to the parochial*   s.5(1)(b) & (3)
church council each year, at the meeting before the annual
parochial church meeting, dealing with the fabric of the
church and the articles belonging to it in the light of the
inspection under (a) and all the actions which have been
taken in the previous year for the protection and maintenance of the fabric and those articles. The report must deal,
in particular, with any action taken to implement the recommendations in a report by the inspecting architect or surveyor under the 1955 Measure; and

(c)   to make the same report (subject to any alterations   s.5(1)(b) & (3)
decided upon by the parochial church council) on the coun-
cil's behalf each year to the *annual parochial church meeting*
of those on a church electoral roll.

29

Here again, the duties apply to each church – defined as in para- s.5(6)
graphs 38-40 – in the parish, and must be carried out separately in
respect of each of them.

59   It is recommended that the report should be a written one,
and that it should be fully discussed both by the parochial church
council and by the annual parochial church meeting. A video film
accompanying a report may be a valuable illustration, but in no way
is it a substitute. It is also recommended that a copy of the report
should be sent to the archdeacon after the annual parochial church
meeting so as to assist in a systematic follow-up to the inspection
reports under the 1955 Measure. The church's inspecting architect
or surveyor should also be kept 'in the picture' at least on a year by
year basis.

60   The churchwardens are, again, to act in consultation with the s.5(2)
minister in carrying out these requirements. By that provision and
the provisions described in paragraph 58, the 1991 Measure ensures
that the minister and parochial church council are all fully informed
on a regular basis of the position as regards the fabric of the church,
the articles belonging to it and the action being taken to care for
them, and that they are all encouraged to co-operate in this aspect
of the life and work of the parish. At the same time, the 1991
Measure ensures that the parochial church council is in a position to
monitor how its legal responsibilities (see para. 14) are being dis-
charged, and that all those on the church electoral roll are kept informed
of the position and given an annual opportunity to discuss it.

Contents of Churches

INSPECTION

61   As explained in paragraph 41(a), the 1991 Measure recognises the importance of the church's contents by bringing any
particular significant, valuable or vulnerable articles within the
scope of the professional inspection and report under the 1955
Measure, and by ensuring that all articles belonging to the church
are covered by the churchwardens' duty to compile and maintain an
inventory and to make an annual inspection and report.

DEPOSIT OF ARTICLES IN PLACES OF SAFETY

62   Valuable articles in churches are often a cause of particular
difficulty and concern to the parish, particularly as thefts from
churches have increased markedly in recent years. The local police
crime prevention officer and the inspecting architect or surveyor
will often be able to give advice on securing some articles unobtru-

sively in their original position and on security marking, although expert advice should of course be taken before marking a valuable article or one of historic interest or before attaching anything permanently to it.

63   Many churches keep valuables such as silver in bank vaults, although deposit in a bank has become more difficult now that the High Street banks are reducing the number of their branches. (Where valuables are deposited in this way, it is strongly recommended that the name under which they are deposited includes a reference to the office held by the person concerned and specifies the parish, and that notice of the deposit is kept with the inventory.) Local or even national museums may be able to take some articles of particular interest, but may not necessarily be able to display them, and transferring them to a museum of course involves moving them into a wholly secular environment.

64   One solution to the problem in some dioceses has been the setting up of cathedral repositories, where church treasures can remain within the guardianship of the Church and yet be on public display in secure conditions. It may also be possible for the church where they originated to borrow them back, subject to suitable conditions, for special occasions. It is recommended that in dioceses where a repository does not already exist the DAC explores the possibility with a view to putting proposals to the diocesan synod and the diocesan board of finance.

65   The 1991 Measure recognises the importance of diocesan repositories by including a power to make rules allowing parochial church councils to deposit articles in approved repositories for safekeeping, after consultation with the DAC but without the need for a faculty. These rules will probably be made fairly soon after the 1991 Measure comes into force, and will need to provide for such matters as the terms and conditions of deposit, as well as safeguards regarding removal, transport and insurance.   s.26(3)(a)

66   In addition, archdeacons are given major new powers to protect articles which belong to churches and which they consider to be of architectural, artistic, historic or archaeological value and exposed to danger of loss or damage. In such a case, an archdeacon who thinks that an article should be removed from the church in order to safeguard it may make an order requiring that to be done, and naming a place of safety to which the article must be moved.   s.21(1)

67   However, this power is subject to safeguards:

(a)   unless the archdeacon considers that the matter is so urgent that the article should be moved to a place of safety immediately, notice of the facts as they appear to the archdeacon must be given to the churchwardens (who will normally have custody of the article), to anyone else who has custody of it, to the parochial church council and to the DAC. The notice must give the recipients at least 28 days to make written representations, and if any representations are made – for example, putting forward proposals for better safeguards for the article in its original position, or making other suggestions as to the place where it should be kept in the future – the archdeacon must give due consideration to them before making the order. If the matter is so urgent that the archdeacon has to act before giving the DAC an opportunity to make representations, the DAC must be informed of what has happened as soon as practicable after the article has been moved to the place of safety; and

s.21(2)

s.21(3)

(b)   within 28 days after the article has been removed to a place of safety in accordance with the archdeacon's order, the archdeacon must apply for a faculty authorising it to be kept there. This again will give all those who have a legitimate interest an opportunity to object and put forward any alternative solutions to the problem.

s.21(6)

68   The archdeacon's order must be in a form prescribed by rules; it is expected that these will be made soon after the 1991 Measure comes into force. The order must also be served on the churchwardens and anyone else who has custody of the article, and if they do not comply with the order the archdeacon may apply to the consistory court for an order compelling them to do so.

s.21(4)

s.21(5)

69   It is recommended that archdeacons exercise this new power sparingly, bearing in mind that once an article is removed from a church it frequently ends up by being sold or disposed of. Where at all possible the archdeacon should seek to have the article made secure in its existing position, or moved to a place of safety, in co-operation with the parish rather than by using the mandatory powers. Except in emergency situations, where notice to the churchwardens, the parochial church council and the DAC is not required (see para. 67(a)), the archdeacon's notice should give a full account of the facts and specific reasons (as opposed to a generalised reference to security problems) for the proposed removal. Where the archdeacon does make an order, it is recommended that this should be done only after taking full advice from the DAC, the

diocesan furnishings officer and, in many cases, the Council for the Care of Churches, as well as other bodies such as local museums, about a suitable place of safety, the best way of removing, transporting and storing the article so as to avoid damage, and also security considerations and insurance. All these factors are of vital importance if the order is to serve its purpose of safeguarding the article, and they will frequently call for specialist advice. Only in an emergency, for example after fire or storm damage, should the archdeacon act without such advice. In any case, it is recommended that the archdeacon makes sure the place to which the article is to be removed is willing to receive it, and that the insurers of the church's contents are notified.

70   Where a parish is faced with a notice from the archdeacon proposing a removal order, it will of course need to consider the matter at once, and take professional advice where necessary on whether and if so how the article can be made secure in its existing position or elsewhere in the church. If that is not possible, and the parish does not agree with the archdeacon's proposals, it is advised, if possible, to put forward positive suggestions as regards the future of the article.

ADDITIONAL CONTENTS AND DISPOSALS

71   The introduction of new articles into the church or the disposal or removal of those which are already there will normally require a faculty, and this subject is dealt with in more detail in Section VI (see para. 201) and Appendix E.

BOOKS AND RECORDS

72   The archdeacon's power to order the removal of an article   s.21(7)
which is described in paragraphs 66-69 does not extend to parochial registers and records. These are subject to a separate system of legal controls and safeguards under the Parochial Registers and Records Measure 1978 ('the 1978 Measure'). The 1978 Measure has recently[8] been amended by the Church of England (Miscellaneous Provisions) Measure 1992,[9] which will, among other things, make it possible to tie in the periodic statutory inspections of registers and records with the cycle of five-yearly inspections of churches under the 1955 Measure. Full details of the 1978 Measure and the new provisions are given in the revised edition of the *Guide to the Parochial Registers and Records Measure 1978* (see Appendix H).

73   In addition, it is expected that rules will be made in the near   s.26(3)(c)
future under the 1991 Measure to provide for the safe-keeping, care,

33

inspection and preservation of books and other documents which do not fall within the scope of the 1978 Measure but which are of historic interest to the Church of England. These rules may, for example, implement the Faculty Jurisdiction Commission's recommendations that each diocese should appoint a diocesan books adviser to oversee the care of books of historic interest which are not covered by existing legislation, and that parochial libraries should be insured by parochial church councils and brought within a five-yearly inspection system parallel to that under the 1978 Measure.[10]

Churchyards

GENERAL

74   The parochial church council's general duty as regards the churchyard is to keep it 'in such an orderly and decent manner as becomes consecrated ground', to keep it duly fenced and to keep the paths clear and in proper order.[11] This is a wide-ranging responsibility, and practical guidance on how to discharge it is provided by the 3rd edition of *The Churchyards Handbook* (see Appendix H). In addition, the 1991 Measure contains specific provisions on two matters – trees and the recording of burials and reserved grave spaces – which are dealt with in detail in paragraphs 83-89 and 90.

75   Although the action which the parochial church council is able to take in this respect will necessarily be limited by the funds and other resources at its disposal, it will need to have a proper plan for the maintenance and management of the churchyard on a long-term as well as a short-term basis, and that plan should be considered by the council and reviewed periodically. It may also be helpful to set up a churchyard committee or appoint a churchyard officer to carry forward the plan on a day to day basis, in collaboration with the minister, although the committee or officer will of course need to report back to the full council and be subject to its directions.

76   The faculty jurisdiction regarding tombstones and memorials in churchyards, and cases where the consistory court has delegated its authority in such matters, are dealt with in detail in paragraphs 208-209. In addition, problems sometimes arise over the maintenance of tombstones and memorials. The primary responsibility for their condition rests with the person who erected the tombstone or memorial; after that person's death, it is generally understood to rest with the heirs of the person commemorated. However, the heirs may not be interested, or may be untraceable, and in any case there is no way of compelling them to maintain the tombstone or memorial, except

possibly where it is a danger to the public. For this reason it may be appropriate to require a donation to the upkeep of the churchyard as a condition for a faculty. If the parochial church council does not maintain tombstones and the like in a safe condition, the council may be liable if someone suffers injury as a result.[12]

77   Where a churchyard has been closed for burials by Order in Council, the Local Government Act 1972[13] lays down a procedure for transferring the parochial church council's responsibilities for the care and maintenance of the churchyard to the local authority. Even where the churchyard has not been formally closed, it may be possible to obtain assistance, financial or otherwise, from the local authority[14] or other public bodies. However, the diocesan registrar should be consulted about any proposal to approach the local authority, so that he can advise on the most suitable legal provisions to use.

78   In any event, the faculty jurisdiction extends to any alterations or additions to consecrated churchyards and some unconsecrated land belonging to churches. Further details are given in Section VI.

WILDLIFE

79   In recent years, there has been a renewed interest in and awareness of the ecological significance of churchyards. Particularly in areas which are predominantly agricultural or urban, churchyards often form a sanctuary for a rich variety of wildlife which has disappeared in the surrounding area, including trees and plants, lichens, insects, birds and a number of species of animals. The churchyard may also be of interest from a geological point of view. It is important that the churchyard is managed in a way that helps to preserve and enhance its character as a wildlife habitat, not only in the interests of the parish but also of the wider community, and the parish's churchyard management plan should take this into account. That aim is not incompatible with making the churchyard visually attractive and ensuring that it appears well cared for. The key to reconciling the two sets of objectives lies in obtaining proper advice; so far as publications are concerned, *The Churchyards Handbook* again contains practical guidance, and an information pack on *The Living Churchyard* which is available from the Church and Conservation Project at the Arthur Rank Centre (see Appendix G), price £6.00 by post, contains a large amount of detailed practical information on a wide range of matters. In addition, advice can be obtained from the local Wildlife Trust, whose address can be obtained from the Royal Society for Nature Conservation (see Appendix G).

80   It is also recommended that DACs which have not already done so should issue guidance to parishes on this aspect of the care of churchyards. For this purpose, they will find it helpful to consult both the Arthur Rank Centre and the local Wildlife Trust. In addition to basic information about management planning and techniques, the guidance could also cover surveys of churchyards, recording information, and making the information available as widely as possible (for example, to local schools).

81   In some cases, discretionary grants are available from English Nature towards the cost of managing the churchyard in the interests of wildlife or special natural features. Here again, details are available from the Arthur Rank Centre or local offices of English Nature.

82   It is possible for the whole or part of a churchyard to be made a Site of Special Scientific Interest,[15] in which case there are statutory obligations to consult English Nature over management. Churches to which this applies will already be aware of the position, as English Nature has a statutory obligation to notify those concerned and liaise with them over management. However, it is more likely that the churchyard may be identified as a site of interest for nature conservation (possibly including a regionally important geological area) on a local plan under the town and country planning legislation,[16] and this may affect any proposal requiring planning permission (see para. 132(a)). The local authority planning department is the obvious source of information here.

TREES IN CHURCHYARDS

83   The 1991 Measure repealed the legislation[17] which gave the Diocesan Parsonages Board a major role in relation to trees in churchyards, and now provides that the parochial church council's powers, duties and liabilities in respect of the care and maintenance of the churchyard are to extend to the trees in it. This expressly includes closed churchyards, and makes it clear that where the local authority takes over the parochial church council's responsibilities in respect of such a churchyard those responsibilities include the trees. The 1991 Measure also recognises the problem that can occur over planting trees – for example, if they are of an unsuitable species or planted in an unsuitable place – by providing that the parochial church council's powers, duties and liabilities extend to trees which it is proposed to plant.   s.6(4)

s.6(1)

s.6(5)

s.6(1)

84   Another new provision in the 1991 Measure ensures that where a tree in a churchyard which is maintainable by the parochial church council is felled, topped or lopped, the council may sell the   s.6(2)

timber or dispose of it in some other way, and is to receive the proceeds, which are to be applied to the maintenance of any church or churchyard which the council is liable to maintain.

85   In the past, some uncertainty has existed as to how far faculties are needed for fairly minor matters involving trees in churchyards for example, removing fairly small self-sown saplings. To help overcome this problem, and to ensure that parochial church councils have guidance on how to fulfil their new responsibilities, the 1991 Measure requires the chancellor, after consultation with the DAC, to give written guidance to all parochial church councils in the diocese on the planting, felling and topping and lopping of trees in churchyards.

s.6(3)

86   In addition to their role in assisting the chancellor to produce diocesan guidance under the Measure, it is recommended that all DACs which have not already done so should produce their own guidance on matters relating to trees in churchyards which the chancellor has not covered. These might, for example, include:

(a) *planting*, including where and where not to plant trees, siting of trees, suitable species, the effects on buildings and archaeology and the best time for planting;

(b) *periodical inspections*, what to look for when they are carried out and remedial measures when problems are discovered;

(c) *tree surgery and felling* (possibly referring to B.S. 3998 – *Recommendations for Tree Works*);

(d) *the effect on trees of building works* (possibly referring to B.S. 5837 – *Guide for Trees in Relation to Construction*);

(e) *trees in hedges*;

(f) *record keeping*; and

(g) *sources of advice* (including local authority tree specialists and conservation officers) and names of suitably qualified professional people available to undertake work in the diocese.

DACs involved in work on these guidelines will find it helpful to see what has been done in other dioceses. Further helpful advice can be obtained from the Church and Conservation Project at the Arthur Rank Centre (see Appendix G).

87   It is also recommended that each diocese considers appointing its own tree adviser, or least indicates in the diocesan year book

37

the names and addresses of the tree specialists appointed by local authorities in the diocese.

88   From the parish's point of view, the proposals for the care of trees need to be integrated into the general plan for the care and maintenance of the churchyard (see para. 75). The parish's first step should be to obtain suitable information and advice – from *The Churchyards Handbook*, from the guidance issued by the chancellor and the DAC, and from the diocesan tree adviser, local authority tree specialist or conservation officer. The parish will also need to check with the local planning authority whether any of the trees in the churchyard are subject to tree preservation orders or whether the churchyard or part of it is in a conservation area; if so, the diocesan registrar should be consulted about the legal effect.

89   It may also be of interest of parishes to know that the results of a survey of yew trees, which are a common feature of older churchyards, is now available from the Yew Tree Campaign at the Conservation Foundation (see Appendix G).

RECORDING OF LOCATIONS OF BURIALS AND RESERVED GRAVE SPACES

90   It is envisaged that rules will be made in the fairly near future   s.26(3)(b)
under the 1991 Measure requiring parochial church councils to keep a record (probably in the form of a plan) of the location of burials in their churchyards and of reserved grave spaces for which faculties have been granted. Many parochial church councils have been doing this for many years – in some cases on the basis of churchyard regulations made by the chancellor (see paras 208-209) or using the guidance and model forms in *The Churchyards Handbook*, or both. All parochial church councils are strongly encouraged to do this as a matter of good practice, even before the rules are made, so far as current burials and reservations are concerned. In particular, this avoids mistakes at a time when bereaved relatives are particularly sensitive to them. In addition, keeping such a plan ties in with the new provision in the Church of England (Miscellaneous Provisions) Measure 1992[18] that as from 1st January 1993 entries in a church's burial register must give a reference number for the burial on a plan.

Ruins

91   The new provisions for the professional inspection of certain ruins in churchyards which are designated by the Council for British Archaeology and the Royal Commission on the Historical Monuments of England as being of outstanding architectural, artistic,

historic or archaeological value have already been explained (see para. 41(b)). These are part of the Church's and the nation's heritage but are usually not directly relevant to the life and mission of the present-day parishes in which they stand. The 1991 Measure there- s.7 fore provides that any expenses which are properly incurred by the parochial church council, with the prior approval of the Diocesan Board of Finance, in implementing a recommendation in an inspection report under the 1955 Measure regarding one of these outstanding ruins are to be refunded by the Board.

Notes

1. 1955 Measure s.1 as amended by the 1991 Measure.

2. 1955 Measure s.1(2)(c).

3. 1955 Measure s.(1); Interpretation Measure 1925 s.3.

4. Care of Cathedrals Measure1990 s.18.

5. 1955 Measure s.2 as amended by the 1991 Measure.

6. Canons E 1, F 13 and F 17.

7. Church Representation Rules r.8.

8. From 1st January 1993.

9. Sch. 1.

10. *The Continuing Care of Churches and Cathedrals,* paras. 137 and 138.

11. Canon F 13; Parochial Church Councils (Powers) Measure 1956 s.4(1)(ii); *Opinions of the Legal Advisory Commission,* 6th ed. p.35.

12. *The Churchyards Handbook* p.42-43; *Opinions of the Legal Advisory Commission,* p.36b-c.

13. s.215.

14. Local Government Act 1972 s.214; Open Spaces Act 1906.

15. Wildlife and Countryside Act 1981 s.28.

16. Town and Country Planning Act 1990 s.36.

17. In Repair of Benefice Buildings Measure 1972 s.20.

18. Sch. 1 para. 11.

IV THE DIOCESAN ADVISORY COMMITTEE

Introduction

92   DACs have existed since the 1920s to provide advice at a
diocesan level, especially to parishes, the chancellor and the archdeacons, in relation to church buildings and other places of worship,
their contents and their churchyards and other land. In particular,
the DACs have developed an important role in advising on faculty
matters and on proposals which will lead to applications for faculties at a later stage; the same, of course, applies in relation to
archdeacons' certificates. DACs were first established on a mandatory basis by the Faculty Jurisdiction Measure 1938,[1] but that
Measure was silent about their constitution, and the Faculty Jurisdiction Measure 1964,[2] which replaced the 1938 Measure, contained only a few very basic provisions regarding their composition
and structure.

93   The 1991 Measure, on the other hand, goes into considerable
detail on these matters. Its main aims so far as DACs are concerned
are three-fold:

(a) to strengthen and extend their advisory role as an essential element in an updated and strengthened faculty jurisdiction system, and to add a new educational role which the DACs are to take the initiative in fulfilling;

(b) to put the DACs in a better position to fulfil those roles by providing for each of them to have a formal written constitution, with the same basic provisions in every diocese, by broadening their membership, and by placing the diocese under a duty to provide them with adequate financial resources for their work; and

(c) to integrate them more closely into the synodical government system at a diocesan level, as well as emphasising their link with parishes on the one hand and their place in a national network of advisory bodies on the other.

Constitution

94   Under the 1991 Measure, the diocesan synod must provide the DAC with a written constitution as soon as practicable, and in any event before 1st March 1996; until it does so, the DAC will continue on the basis of the Faculty Jurisdiction Measure 1964, and it is recommended that the diocesan synod makes the new DAC constitution a priority. The constitution is to contain the provisions set out in Schedule 1 to the 1991 Measure or 'provisions to the like effect'. It is considered that these last words allow the diocese to use its own wording for the constitution, although the use of the statutory wording is strongly recommended. To a very limited extent, it may also bring in matters of a purely local nature which are not inconsistent with Schedule 1 (see for example para. 96(c)), but it should not normally be necessary to write these into the constitution, and the diocese is recommended to cover them in other ways (see again para. 96(c)) so far as at all possible. In any event, the diocesan synod cannot alter the basic provisions of the Schedule itself, for example by reducing the minimum number of members, changing the bodies involved in appointing them or changing their terms of office.

s.2(2)
s.2(4)

s.2(8)

s.2(2)

NAME

95   The formal name of the Committee is to be the [name of diocese] Diocesan Advisory Committee.

Sch.1
para.1

MEMBERSHIP

96   The DAC must consist of:

41

(a) *the chairman*, who is appointed by the bishop after consultation with the bishop's council, the chancellor and the Council for the Care of Churches. It is recommended that the process of appointment should take the form of a genuine dialogue with all these people and bodies, rather than merely submitting a single name for comment;

Sch.1
paras 2&3

(b) *all the archdeacons in the diocese* Their membership of the Diocesan Advisory Committee is an integral part of the archdeacon's enhanced role under the 1991 Measure; and

Sch.1
para.2

(c) *at least twelve other members* Of these, two are to be appointed elected members of the diocesan synod, in order to strengthen the relationship between the two bodies (see para. 93(c)), and at least ten are to be appointed by the bishop's council; in the case of one after consultation with English Heritage, in the case of another after consultation with the National Amenity Societies (see para. 26), and in the case of a third after consultation with 'the relevant associations of local authorities'. (The bodies at present designated by the Dean of the Arches as 'relevant associations of local authorities' are the Association of Metropolitan Authorities, the Association of County Councils and the Association of District Councils – the addresses and telephone numbers of all these bodies appear in Appendix G.) In making the appointments, it is recommended that the bishop's council should, again, conduct a genuine dialogue with the bodies to be consulted, and it must also ensure that those appointed have, between them, knowledge of the history, development and use of church buildings; knowledge of the liturgy and worship of the Church of England; knowledge of architecture, archaeology, art and history; and experience in the care of historic buildings and their content. These requirements tie in with the basic principles explained in Section I of this Code, and it is recommended that consultation again takes place with the Council for the Care of Churches in order to help find the best qualified members. Even if the written constitution of the particular Committee does not expressly provide for it, the bishop's council may also wish to look for knowledge in additional spheres, for example wildlife, and also knowledge of a local nature, for example of local history, architecture and craftsmanship. The question of expert members, who are essential in view of the nature of the

Sch.1
paras 1&4

Sch.1
para.5

Committee's functions (see paras 108-111), is considered in the following paragraph.

97   The precise number of members appointed by the bishop's council will depend on such factors as the size of the diocese, the volume of faculty work, the proposed sub-committee structure (see paras 101-102) and the minimum number of people needed to represent the necessary range of knowledge and expertise. It is also possible for the Committee itself with the bishop's consent, to co-opt additional members (provided the number of co-opted members does not rise above one-third of the number of the other members). In addition, the Committee may request the bishop to appoint suitably qualified consultants. In general, the Council for the Care of Churches recommends that the status of consultant is given only sparingly, on the basis that it is better to encourage experts to spread their informed knowledge throughout the whole of the Committee's business, by making them full members, than to keep them in a secondary category, and this is particularly important in fulfilling the Committee's non-faculty work, which may often require an input from several different specialists for a single project. However, in a large diocese, it may well be necessary to have more than one person to give specialist advice on a particular matter (such as, for example, organs or heating), so that no one person is faced with an unreasonable volume of requests to visit parishes over a wide geographical area. (As regards visits, see paras 103 and 117 and Appendix A Part III para. 2.) *[margin: Sch.1 para.12 Sch.1 para.13]*

98   Apart from the archdeacons, members of DACs are not required by the 1991 Measure to be practising members of the Church of England, or even Christians. However, it is essential that they are committed to implementing the Measure, including the general principles which underlie it or which it specifically lays down; thus all of them have to have regard to s.1 of the 1991 Measure (see para. 3).

99   The 1991 Measure also contains detailed provisions as regards the term of office of the chairman and other appointed members (normally six years), the dates of initial appointments after the 1991 Measure comes into force, and matters such as casual vacancies. *[margin: Sch.1 paras 6 & 7 Sch.1 paras 8-11]*

PROCEDURE AND SUB-COMMITTEES

100   The 1991 Measure expressly permits the diocesan synod to add its own provisions on procedure or sub-committees to the DAC's written constitution. So far as procedure is concerned, it is recommended that the constitution fixes the quorum for meetings and permits the DAC to regulate its own procedure so far as that is not expressly laid down by the constitution. *[margin: s.2(3)]*

101   The sub-committee structure which is adopted will depend very much on the requirements of the particular diocese and the way in which the particular DAC has traditionally operated. The Faculty Jurisdiction Commission suggested as alternatives a standing committee or a sub-committee for each area or archdeaconry (which may be particularly useful for a large diocese). In each case the members of the sub-committee or sub-committees should be drawn from the membership of the main Committee and should reflect its composition. It is recommended that the scope of each sub-committee's delegated authority is clearly laid down, and decisions of the sub-committees should be recorded in writing and reported to the full Committee.

102   In addition, the increasing amount of business of DACs generally requires careful attention to be given to the Committee's procedure and agenda. In most dioceses it will probably be helpful to have a small sub-committee, serviced by the secretary and consisting of the chairman, one or more archdeacons and one or more professional people from among the appointed members (for example, an architect), to scrutinise the business a week or so before the full Committee meets. The sub-committee can look at the bulk of relatively standard applications, such as repairs recommended in reports under the 1955 Measure, and can recommend advice on these cases which can then be listed for 'en bloc' approval by the full Committee, although members would of course have the right to request discussion of any particular item. The sub-committee can also highlight potentially controversial cases so that time can be reserved at the meeting of the full Committee to discuss them properly, and a paper can be circulated explaining the background. The sub-committee can also help prioritise the agenda of meetings of the full Committee by focusing on particular subjects to be dealt with. All this will help to ensure that meetings of the full Committee are as efficient, brief and interesting as possible, which in turn will help to ensure that voluntary members are willing to continue serving, and that routine faculty business does not 'take over' the agenda to the detriment of other matters.

103   A further task for a sub-committee might be to co-ordinate an adequate programme of visits, which again are vital if the DAC is to reach informed decisions. (See also para. 117 and Appendix A Part III para. 2).

THE SECRETARY

104   The secretary of the DAC must be appointed by the bishop after consultation with the chairman of the DAC and the chief administrative officer of the diocese (normally the diocesan secre-

Sch.1
para.14

tary). The qualifications needed and terms of appointment will vary from one diocese to another, depending on what other duties, if any, the secretary is required to perform, but it is recommended that a clear job description is always drawn up.

105   In many dioceses, the task of acting as secretary to the DAC is seen as one of the senior administrative tasks of the full-time diocesan secretariat, and may be one of the functions to be performed by the diocesan secretary or an assistant diocesan secretary. Where this is so, the necessary resources by way of secretarial assistance and other facilities will probably be in place. Where the work is to be carried out by someone outside the central administration of the diocese, it is essential for the diocese to make sure that the secretary has adequate resources for his or her work.

106   It is recommended that the secretary's basic task should be to deal with the day-to-day and year by year administration of the DAC, such as the matters set out in paragraph 16 of the Model Code of Business and Procedure in Part III of Appendix A to this Code (see para. 120) except so far as they are provided for in some other way. In addition, the secretary will need to keep the register of s.15(3) faculty petitions required by the 1991 Measure and ensure that it is open to public inspection (see para. 152), and it is recommended that copies of the DAC's agendas are kept with the register. The secretary Sch.3 will also receive copies of reports under the 1955 Measure (see para. 43).   para.2(b)

107   Apart from statutory functions, the Secretary may be called upon to give evidence as a judge's witness at hearings before the consistory court, and he or she will also need to brief other members of the DAC when they are required to give evidence. The secretary also has a leading part to play in fulfilling the DAC's educational role, and in fostering good relations with DAC members, other diocesan staff, parishes and all those involved in the care of churches. Those wishing to obtain a faculty should be encouraged to contact the secretary at as early a stage as possible, and while their proposals are still in the formative stage, for informal preliminary advice (see para. 122(d)).

Functions

108   The work which the 1991 Measure places at the forefront of Sch.2 the DAC's activities is still its advisory role; it is not intended to be para.1(a) a quasi-judicial body nor an enforcement agency for the faculty jurisdiction. The DAC is required 'to act as an advisory body on matters affecting places of worship and, in particular, to give advice when requested . . . ' to any of the people or bodies listed later in this paragraph 'on matters relating to:

45

(a)   the grant of faculties;

(b)   the architecture, archaeology, art and history of places of worship;

(c)   the use, care, planning and redundancy of places of worship;

(d)   the use and care of the contents of such places; and

(e)   the use and care of churchyards and burial grounds.'

This is obviously a very wide brief, much more so than under the Faculty Jurisdiction Measure 1964, and a list of people and bodies who may request the DAC's advice is also a long one, covering the bishop, the chancellor, the archdeacons, parochial church councils, intending applicants for faculties, the diocesan pastoral committee and those who are engaged in the planning, design and building of new places of worship in the diocese which are not within the jurisdiction of the consistory court. In addition, the DAC has power to respond to requests for advice from any other persons where the Committee thinks it appropriate to do so.

Sch.2
para.2(a)-(g)

Sch.2
para.2(h)

109   Quite apart from all these provisions, the Faculty Jurisdiction Rules urge all applicants for faculties (with very few exceptions) to seek the DAC's formal advice before lodging the petition (see paras 141-145), and the 1991 Measure requires the chancellor and the archdeacons to seek the DAC's formal advice (again with very few exceptions) before taking a final decision on faculty matters (see paras 167 and 176). However, as will be seen from the previous paragraph, the DAC's advisory role extends far beyond faculty matters, or matters which may become faculty matters in the future; to give one example which is not specifically mentioned in the 1991 Measure, the wording in relation to the care of churchyards is clearly wide enough to cover the wildlife aspects (see paras 79-80). Because of that, it is important that the pressure of routine faculty business is not allowed to dominate the Committee's agenda to such an extent that other requests for advice cannot properly be considered. Moreover, the Committee is not limited to giving advice on request. It can take the initiative when it sees that is needed, and is recommended to do so; this is of course bound up with its educational role.

FJR r.3

s.15(1)&(2)

110   In addition, the DAC is given a number of other functions, most although not all of them introduced for the first time by the 1991 Measure. The Measure itself sets out the essential functions of the DACs in a Schedule which is reproduced in Part I of Appendix A to this Code. However, the diocesan synod may also resolve that

Sch.2
para.1(b)-(g)

46

the Committee should have additional functions, and it is recommended that consideration is given to some or all of the additional functions drawn from the Faculty Jurisdiction Commission's report which are set out in Part II of Appendix A; the bishop or the chancellor may also request the Committee to perform additional functions. `Sch.2 para.1(g)` `Sch.2 para.1(g)`

111   All these functions are important, and they are all ones the DAC must take the initiative in fulfilling. However, a few call for special mention:

(a) 'to take action to encourage the care and appreciation of places of worship, churchyards and burial grounds and the contents of such places, and for that purpose to publicise methods of conservation, repair, construction, adaptation and re-development'. Thus, the Committee's educational role is specifically laid down by the 1991 Measure, and its very broad terms include, for example, aspects such as archaeology (mentioned elsewhere in the 1991 Measure) and the wildlife of churchyards. One way in which the Committee can fulfil this function is by publishing guidelines on general and particular aspects of its work for circulation in the diocese, but there are many others, some of which are mentioned in paragraphs 116-117; and `Sch.2 para.1(f)`

(b) to keep in touch with the Council for the Care of Churches and other official bodies and amenity societies and to conduct discussions and negotiations with other professional and other organisations. This is a summary of parts of the 'additional' functions in the Faculty Jurisdiction Commission report, and the activities it includes are covered in more detail in paragraphs 118-119.

Guiding Principles

112   In carrying out all these functions, the DAC and its members must of course be committed to the general principles of the 1991 Measure, as explained in Section I of this Code. The Measure specifically requires the Committee and any sub-committees to have regard to the rites and ceremonies of the Church of England; this is an obvious aspect of the general requirement to have due regard to the church's role as a local centre of worship and mission. `s.2(5)` `s.1`

The Position of Members

113   Members of DACs are not delegates or representatives of either the body which appointed them or any other body which was consulted about their appointment, although they are encouraged to

report back to those bodies and to keep them interested in and informed of the Committee's activities. Members must exercise an independent judgement on each matter before them, must declare any interest and withdraw from the discussion in appropriate cases, and must exercise reasonable care and (in the case of professional people) reasonable professional skill and judgement. Dioceses are recommended to contact the Council for the Care of Churches about insurance for members.

Resources

114 The 1991 Measure also lays down for the first time the general principle that any expense incurred in providing the DAC with a written constitution or incurred so as to enable it to discharge its functions properly and effectively are to be paid by the Diocesan Board of Finance, provided the Board has approved them beforehand. This makes it clear that each diocese, through its Diocesan Board of Finance, must make adequate funds available for the work of the DAC. In particular, it is important to provide realistic remuneration for the secretary and other staff, to cover essential office expenses and to provide proper facilities for meetings (for example, equipment for displaying plans and drawings). It is also essential to provide for members's expenses, bearing in mind that nowadays few of them are likely to be able to meet travelling and other expenses from their own pockets.

s.2(6)

115 Each diocese will have its own budgetary arrangements. In the majority, mechanisms will already exist for the DAC's annual budget to be prepared, scrutinised and approved, but when they do not, it is recommended that the chief administrative officer ensures that the appropriate budgetary process is established and that, where necessary, the secretary of the Committee is offered advice on the drawing up of budgets. The diocese may also have a forward budget planned for, say, three years ahead, kept up on a rolling programme, and here again it is recommended that the DAC's budget is integrated with it.

The DAC's Place in the Life of the Diocese and Liaison with other Bodies

116 At diocesan level, the role of the bishop, the bishop's council, the diocesan synod and the Diocesan Board of Finance in making appointments, designating additional functions for the DAC and providing it with finance have already been described (see paras 96, 104, 110 and 114). In addition, the 1991 Measure requires the DAC to prepare an annual report and lay it before the diocesan synod, with a copy going to the Council for the Care of Churches. However, personal contact is also vital; hence the provision in the 1991

s.1(7)

Measure requiring two members of the Committee to be drawn from the elected members of the diocesan synod. In addition, it is recommended that the DAC takes advantage of any opportunity to make oral reports on its work to that synod. It should of course maintain liaison with other diocesan bodies and officers whose work interlocks with its own – for example, the Diocesan Pastoral Committee, the Diocesan Liturgical or Worship Committee, the Diocesan Redundant Churches Uses Committee and the Furnishings Officer. Further, it is recommended that its activities are publicised in the diocesan newsletter, and that its annual report is published as part of any diocesan annual report which is produced, as well as ensuring that its agenda are available for public inspection at the same place as the statutory register of faculty petitions (see para. 106). Regular meetings – say at least once a year – with the bishop and the chancellor are also recommended.

Sch.1
para.4(a)

117 So far as the relationship with deaneries and parishes is concerned, personal contact is again essential, and it is recommended that members and the secretary should seek out opportunities for such contact in the ways suggested in this paragraph. One obvious example is that where a parish has submitted proposals to the DAC for advice one or more members will frequently need to visit the parish and report back to the full Committee before it takes its final decision. Members and the secretary are recommended to accept – and indeed encourage – invitations to speak at deanery synods and meetings of parochial church councils. It is suggested that the DAC should introduce itself and its range of activities to new incumbents, preferably by letter, should organise or participate in 'training days' for incumbents and churchwardens, and should produce an annual leaflet for parishes with details of dates of meetings and closing dates for applications, together with general procedural advice and topical material. Quite apart from all this, the archdeacon should act as a link between the DAC and the parish, both at formal occasions such as visitations and informally during pastoral work (see para. 20); the archdeacon should endeavour to convince the parishes that the DAC is their friend and adviser, rather than a judge or a policeman.

118 The DACs are also part of a national network of advisory bodies. They do not work in isolation, and should take positive steps to strengthen their links with neighbouring DACs and the Council for the Care of Churches. In addition to regional meetings, neighbouring DACs may be able to collaborate, for example in contacts with professionals along the lines described in paragraphs 35 and 119 and in drawing up guidelines on particular subjects such as wildlife or archaeology. There are links with the Council for the

Care of Churches on specific faculty matters, but they can only work successfully where they are supported by regular contact. The Council sends out at least two newsletters a year to DACs as well as holding an annual conference, and in addition to sending the Council a copy of the Committee's annual report, as required by the 1991 Measure, it is recommended that the secretary also sends in copies of agenda, minutes and supporting reports; this is intended as an aid to dialogue and exchange of information, not an attempt by the Council to control the Committee's activities or decisions. DACs are also encouraged to keep the Council for the Care of Churches informed about matters of general and particular concern in the diocese, just as the Council keeps the DACs informed of national developments.

s.2(7)

119 The DAC should seek to foster close links with relevant professional bodies, for example by organising or joining in regular conferences or seminars. This is, of course, in addition to the DAC's specific role in relation to architects and surveyors who are appointed to inspect and report under the 1955 Measure. It is also most important for the DAC to maintain a close and friendly relationship with the local planning authorities in the diocese, with both local and national amenity societies and with other national bodies, conservation societies and trusts. These bodies seek to fulfil many of the same basic aims as the DAC's; there will rightly be difference of emphasis and outlook between the DAC and the secular bodies, which each have their own particular concerns, but close contact will help to keep any problems to a minimum. In particular, many of the DACs already send their agendas and minutes to the National Amenity Societies; the Societies value this greatly as a means of ensuring that their participation in the faculty proceedings is effective, timely, well-informed and constructive, and all DACs are strongly recommended to adopt the same practice.

Model Code of Business and Procedure

120 Finally, in addition to the specific provisions of the 1991 Measure, it is recommended that in general DACs prepare and follow a Code of Business and Procedure based on the Model Code in Appendix 5 to the Faculty Jurisdiction Commission report, updated to take account of the 1991 Measure and Rules. An updated version of the Model Code along these lines is set out in Part III of Appendix A to this Code, and members and secretaries of DACs are encouraged to study it and make use of it to prepare their own versions.

Notes

1. s.5   2. s.13

V   REPAIRS, ALTERATIONS AND ADDITIONS TO CHURCHES, THEIR CONTENTS AND CHURCHYARDS – THE PRELIMINARY STEPS

Preliminary Steps and Consultation

121   Where a parish wishes to carry out repair or other work, or to make additions or alterations to the church, its contents or the church-yard (including disposals and other transactions), the initial stages in the project are vital, whether it be large or small. Nothing can guarantee a trouble-free progress and eventual success for proposals which have controversial elements, but following the proper procedure and carrying out initial consultations before the details are finalised are almost certain to save time, trouble and money later, and this applies equally to non-controversial projects. In particular, parishes are strongly recommended to consult widely when embarking on major schemes such as extensions or large-scale reordering, and to ensure that their architects produce alternative sketch plans for discussion, so as to make it clear that different ideas are being considered, and that they are not merely considering a single scheme which will be pursued whatever the responses to it.

122   It is therefore recommended that:

(a)   there should, as a first step, be wide-ranging consult-ation within the parish, so as to obtain a consensus if at all possible, and this should be followed by a written statement setting out in general terms what is proposed. If it seems that the proposals are not gaining general acceptance, it is im-portant to ensure that they have not been misunderstood; for example, it may be helpful in some cases to convene a meeting open to all parishioners where the proposals can be explained and discussed;

(b)   at an early stage, the parish should also consult the archdeacon, although if the proposals are ones which may

51

fall within the archdeacon's own faculty jurisdiction (see para. 162 and Appendix D) he may not be able to become as deeply involved as in cases where the faculty application will go to the chancellor in any event;

(c)   similarly, the parish should at an early stage seek appropriate professional advice. It should generally consult the church's inspecting architect or surveyor, and may also need specialist advice. Among other materials, it is recommended that the parish's professional advisers take account of *Department of the Environment Circular 8/87* (on Historic Buildings and Conservation Areas), which contains useful technical advice on repairs to historic buildings and considerations to be taken into account in deciding the appropriateness of alterations or extensions, and also English Heritage's *Policy Statement on New Work in Historic Churches*; and

(d)   there should always be informal consultation with the DAC, through its secretary, and the Committee should always be willing to send representatives to discuss embryonic ideas, however minor.

In all these cases, it is obviously important that there should be close liaison between the archdeacon, the DAC and also the diocesan registrar, who will be consulted on legal points. All of them should make every effort to be seen as approachable, so that the parish feels comfortable about asking for guidance at an early stage.

123   In addition, there are a number of other bodies which may also need to be consulted early on. It is recommended that the relevant National Amenity Society or Societies, English Heritage and the local planning authority should all be brought in at an early stage, especially if they may be involved formally later, for example under r.12(3) of the Faculty Jurisdiction Rules or in a case of total or partial demolition (see paras 172 and 194(c)). If there is any doubt as to which is the appropriate National Amenity Society, the parish should begin by contacting the Joint Committee of the National Amenity Societies (see Appendix G). English Heritage should always be consulted at an early stage if its subsequent approval may be needed at a later stage under grant conditions (see para. 135), or if it may be formally involved in the faculty proceedings, for example under r.12(3) of the Faculty Jurisdiction Rules or in a case of total or partial demolition (see paras 172 and 194(c)). In addition, there are cases where it is important to contact the Commonwealth War Graves Commission, archaeological bodies or

wildlife bodies at the outset, and these are dealt with in the following paragraphs.

124   As regards war graves and memorials with which the Commonwealth War Graves Commission (see Appendix G) is concerned, there are more of these in churches, churchyards and burial grounds than is generally appreciated. In addition to the war graves marked by its own familiar war pattern headstone, the Commission is also responsible for many other war graves and memorials, some outside the normally accepted dates of the First and Second World Wars and some marked by private memorials (of various types and sizes) provided by families. Difficulties can arise because these are not readily identifiable as war graves. Thus where there are any plans involving disturbance of human remains or memorials those concerned should, at the earliest possible opportunity, contact the Commission. It can assist by confirming, from its own definitive records, whether its interests are likely to be affected and by indicating any special requirement. Early consultation in this way should generally ensure that the respective needs of the parish, the Commonwealth War Graves Commission and anyone else can be met, thus easing the passage of subsequent proceedings and, in particular, any subsequent faculty petition.

125   Turning to archaeology, it is important to appreciate that this is not concerned only with buried features. Church archaeology involves the complete study of the fabric of the church, both above and below ground, together with its contents and its historic setting. The whole entity constitutes a valuable historical resource and is central to the community, whether churchgoers or not, which it has served. Even fairly minor works within the church or its churchyard may affect archaeological remains, and it is important that these are considered at an early stage. Among the works which are particularly 'sensitive' in this respect are cleaning, replastering or replacement of ancient wall surfaces, structural repairs, relaying of floors and insertion of heating systems, as well as the more obvious works that disturb the ground, such as the digging of external channels and the work of drain maintenance, disturbance to the churchyard, extensions, new boiler houses, immersion fonts and underground rooms.

126   The DAC may have produced guidelines on the subject, and if so they should be followed. In all cases the parish should begin by contacting the Diocesan Archaeological Adviser if there is one, or if there is none by obtaining the name of a suitable archaeologist from the DAC. If the Archaeological Adviser or archaeologist advises that the project does in fact have archaeological implica-

tions, the parish will need to obtain and pay for a brief report from an archaeological body approved by the DAC, although the cost should normally be modest. The report may be able to identify ways of minimising or avoiding disturbance of archaeological remains through minor modifications to the plans, for example the sensitive use of foundations, and this is desirable if at all possible. The report will need to accompany the application for formal approval to the DAC when the parish reaches that stage (see para. 141). Where nationally important archaeological remains are thought to exist, the expectation must be that they will need to be preserved in their existing position. Even in less sensitive cases the DAC may recommend that the remains be preserved or that the parish be required to arrange for recording or a full excavation by an approved archaeologist or archaeological body before the work commences. Funds may be available to help with the cost, and the archdeacon and the DAC should be asked to advise on this. Where insufficient is known about the archaeology of the site, the DAC may require the parish to have a formal assessment carried out, and base its recommendations on the result. (As regards the Council for British Archaeology, see para. 26(b)).

127   So far as wildlife is concerned, paragraph 79 explains the importance of churchyards in this respect, but works to the church itself may also affect, for example, lichens and the habitat of birds and bats. Whenever there is a possibility that the proposals would have an impact on wildlife the parish should approach the local Wildlife Trust (see para. 79), the local authority conservation officer or English Nature (see Appendix G) to suggest an ecologist to examine the proposals, make suggestions and prepare a brief report which can be submitted to the DAC. It may be possible for ecologists to provide this service free of charge as part of their normal work, although where that is not possible parishes will need to meet the ecologists' charges. Here again, the ecologist may be able to suggest minor modifications to the plan which will minimise or remove the danger of disturbance without affecting the basic project. Where there is a possibility that the proposal may fall within the scope of the Wildlife and Countryside Act 1981 (see para. 134), English Nature should in any case be consulted as soon as possible.

Special Cases

128   The first part of this Section of the Code envisages that the proposal will have originated with the parish, and that the parish is carrying it forward. Where that is not the case, the project will normally fall into one of two categories:

(a) *proposals for a donor to give something to the church* In this case the best course is for the parochial church council to discuss the idea as soon as it is put forward, decide whether it wishes to support the project, and if so see that the consultations outlined in the previous paragraphs take place in the ordinary way. An early discussion with a prospective donor may also help the donor to consider whether the gift offered is appropriate to the church. There may be an alternative gift which has not occurred to the donor but which the parish would welcome and which, if given in memory of a particular person, would make a more suitable form of commemoration (see also Appendix E);

(b) *proposals for tombstones or memorials, reserved grave spaces or exhumation of human remains* In many cases a tombstone or memorial which complies with standards approved by the chancellor can be dealt with without the need for a faculty (see paras 208-209) and without any extensive prior consultation. Where what is proposed is non-standard, the parochial church council should again be consulted and take a view of the proposal, and the person who wishes to erect the tombstone or monument should be encouraged to consult the archdeacon and the DAC at an early stage. Special rules apply to reservation of grave spaces and exhumation (see paras 199-200), and anyone who raises such a possibility should be advised to consult the diocesan registrar without delay. In any case, the parish should consider whether what is suggested may involve disturbance of archaeological remains or war graves or memorials and, if so, urge the person who has put forward the proposals to seek appropriate advice (see paras 124-126).

129   There are also cases where repairs or other work are necessary as a matter of urgency. In that event, the parish should obtain advice from its inspecting architect or surveyor on the degree of the urgency, and should carry out all the consultations recommended above, albeit on a shortened time-scale, except in so far as they are advised that the emergency is such that this might be to the detriment of the church itself or its contents.

Finalising the Proposals and Dealing with Legal Requirements other than Faculties

130   The next stage, after the preliminary consultations, will be for the parochial church council to finalise the proposals, obtain any

necessary professional specifications, drawings and other documentation to show precisely what is intended, and to obtain quotations or estimates for the cost. The inspecting architect or surveyor should normally be closely involved throughout the process. Finally, the parochial church council should pass a formal resolution approving the detailed proposals. Where the initiative for the proposal does not come from within the parochial church council but, for example, from a potential donor (see para. 128(a)), it will be for that person to obtain the specifications, drawings and information about cost, but the parochial church council will normally need to pass a formal resolution either supporting the proposal, opposing it or taking a neutral position. (This will not normally be necessary in the case of 'standard' tombstones and memorials, and in the case of exhumation and reservation of grave spaces the diocesan registrar should be approached for advice on the course the parochial church council should take.)

131   Once this has been done, and before launching into the procedure under the Faculty Jurisdiction Rules, the parochial church council (or anyone else initiating the proposals) will also need to consider whether there are any other legal requirements which have to be satisfied and, in particular, whether any permission apart from a faculty is required. The main requirements of this kind are set out in the following paragraphs.

132   First come requirements under the secular legislation relating to planning, listed buildings, conservation areas, ancient monuments, trees and related subjects. The 1991 Measure contains a s.31(6) specific provision making it clear that nothing in the Measure overrides or affects these aspects of the secular law. Taking them in turn:

(a) *planning permission*   It is sometimes thought that Church of England churches have a 'blanket' exemption from the ordinary legislation on planning permission, but this is not the case, although the ordinary exceptions which apply to secular buildings may be applicable. Where what is proposed involves building or engineering work or other operations of any kind, even of a minor nature (except those which do not affect the exterior of the building), or where there is to be a change in the use of a building or land, the inspecting architect or surveyor and the diocesan registrar should be asked for advice and, if necessary, the local planning authority should be consulted on the need for planning permission;[1]

(b) *listed building consent* In general, any works which involve the demolition of a listed building, or its alteration or extension in a manner that would affect its character as a building of special architectural or historic interest, require listed building consent.[2] There is a special 'ecclesiastical exemption' for ecclesiastical buildings which are for the time being used for ecclesiastical purposes.[3] In a Written Answer in the House of Commons on 17th December 1992 the Secretary of State for National Heritage announced his intention to make a number of changes in the current provisions on this exemption; these would include restricting the exemption to the principal place of worship on any site, as opposed to other buildings within the curtilage, but the Secretary of State confirmed that the precise implications for the withdrawal of the exemption for curtilage buildings including such structures as tombstones and monuments would be discussed further with the Churches, the local authority associations and the National Amenity Societies.[4] The implications of this announcement as regards Church of England churches are under discussion with the Department of National Heritage;

(c) *conservation area consent* In general, a building in a conservation area may not be demolished without conservation area consent (subject to a similar exemption to that in (b) above);[5]

(d) *scheduled monument consent* In general, works affecting scheduled ancient monuments require scheduled monument consent.[6] An ecclesiastical building for the time being used for ecclesiastical purposes cannot be scheduled as an ancient monument,[7] but this exemption is not treated as excluding a monument which is in a churchyard but distinct from the church itself (for example a churchyard cross or a ruin) or a separate monument in the form of archaeological remains (such as a Roman fort) lying beneath the church or churchyard;

(e) *tree preservation orders and trees in conservation areas* In the case of a tree preservation order, precisely what acts affecting the tree require consent from the local authority depend on the terms of the individual order, and this will need to be checked with the local planning authority.[8] There are also restrictions on acts affecting trees which are not subject to tree preservation orders but which stand in conservation areas;[9] and

(f) *control of advertisements* This is of particular importance in relation to church notice boards, and full details are given in *The Churchyards Handbook.*[10]

133   In all these cases, it is recommended that if consent is needed under the secular legislation it is obtained first, while maintaining close contact with the DAC and the archdeacon. If the secular authorities require any modifications to the proposals, they can then be worked in before formal approval is requested from the DAC and a petition for a faculty is submitted, thus saving time and money which might otherwise have been wasted if the faculty proceedings had been taken first, and helping to secure a final result which is acceptable to all concerned. On the other hand, if the secular permission cannot be obtained, and the project cannot go ahead, the additional expense of faculty proceedings can then be avoided. (After any necessary permission or consent under the headings in the previous paragraph, and a faculty, have been obtained, the parish's architect or surveyor will also need to deal with the building regulations requirements where they apply).

134   As regards wildlife, the Wildlife and Countryside Act 1981 includes provisions for the protection of wild birds, their eggs and nests which are in use or being built,[11] certain protected species of wild plants,[12] and also protected species of wild animals, including bats.[13] There are certain special exemptions, depending on the type of wild life involved. However, if a church has bats or even has a history of roosting bats, there is a legal obligation under the 1981 Act to consult English Nature (see Appendix G) before undertaking any action that may affect the bats or their roosts; such action includes timber treatment as well as structural repairs. This requirement must also be dealt with before the faculty petition is completed.

135   English Heritage grants for repairs (and those given by its predecessor in this respect, the Department of the Environment, from 1977 to 1984) contain the following condition, agreed with the General Synod Office:

No works of addition, alteration or redecoration or works not eligible for grant aid will be carried out at any time from the date of this letter (except for maintenance and minor repair works and works required for liturgical purposes which are compatible with the historic character and appearance of the building and which are reversible) without the prior written consent of English Heritage. This is in order that English Heritage may be satisfied that the works will not damage the fabric and fittings or impair the historic and architectural fabric of the building, for the maintenance of which the grant has been offered.

English Heritage is currently reviewing all its grants conditions and will look at this particular wording in the light of the operation of these rules. Parishes who have received grants from either the Department of the Environment or English Heritage should therefore continue to seek the written approval of English Heritage, as well as any other permissions. Although there is no requirement to repay the grant if approval is not received, English Heritage grants are discretionary and dependent on the building and contents remaining of 'outstanding' architectural or historical interest. It is therefore in the parish's long-term best interests to ensure that nothing is done to affect the grant eligibility of the church building and its contents.

Notes

1. Town and Country Planning Act 1990 s.55

2. Planning (Listed Buildings and Conservation Areas) Act 1990 s.7-8.

3. Planning (Listed Buildings and Concervation Areas) Act 1990 s.60.

4. Hansard, House of Commons, 17th December 1992, col. 370-371.

5. Planning (Listed Buildings and Conservation Areas) Act 1990 s.74-75.

6. Ancient Monuments and Archaeological Areas Act 1979 s.2.

7. Ancient Monuments and Archaeological Areas Act 1979 s.61(8).

8. Town and Country Planning Act 1990 s.198.

9. Town and Country Planning Act 1990 s.211.

10. p.72.

11. s.1.

12. s.13.

13. s.9 and Sch.5.

VI THE FACULTY JURISDICTION –
PRACTICE AND PROCEDURE

Introduction

136   This Section describes the normal course of a faculty petition
under the 1991 Measure and the Faculty Jurisdiction Rules. It is
necessarily fairly technical, because it deals with technical procedural matters. However, the rules were made to ensure that the final

decision is taken on the basis of full information about the proposals and the circumstances as a whole, and that anyone with a legitimate interest has a proper opportunity to voice his or her own views. The faculty procedure, unlike some cases in the secular courts, is not a contest between two opposing sides but an attempt to reach the best possible decision. Complying with the legal requirements inevitably takes a certain amount of time and trouble, but it is time and trouble well spent in the interests of the Church and the wider community, and it will also help to avoid delays and complications because of procedural problems at a later stage. Indeed, the 1991 Measure and the Rules themselves are intended to keep the expense and delay in obtaining a faculty to a minimum.

Is a Faculty Necessary?

137   Once there are firm proposals 'on the table', set out in detailed plans, drawings and other documentation and accompanied by clear details of the cost, the next stage is to establish whether or not it is necessary to apply for a faculty. The following paragraphs set out the basic tests, but if there is any doubt about the position the diocesan registrar should always be consulted.

138   In general, and subject to some exceptions which are explained in the following paragraphs, a faculty is required from the chancellor or the archdeacon to authorise works, additions or alterations to or transactions affecting: s.11(1)

(a)   *any parish church, its churchyard and the articles belonging to it*   The 1991 Measure makes it clear that the faculty jurisdiction applies to all parish churches, whether or not they have previously claimed to be 'peculiars' and thus exempt from the jurisdiction of the bishop and the consistory court. However, parish church cathedrals are not included unless they have 'opted' for the faculty jurisdiction under the Care of Cathedrals Measure 1990;[1]

(b)   *other consecrated buildings and other land within the faculty jurisdiction*, including unconsecrated land which forms or is within the curtilage of a church covered by the faculty jurisdiction.[2] Guidance as to the meaning of 'curtilage' in this context is given in the Opinions of the Legal Advisory Commission;[3] (It should be noted that some consecrated buildings other than parish churches *are* 'peculiars' and are not within the faculty jurisdiction.)

61

(c) *buildings which have not been consecrated but were licensed for public worship before 1st March 1993, and which the bishop has expressly brought within the faculty jurisdiction*[4] The bishop's direction here includes the furnishings and contents of the building, and may be made even after the 1991 Measure comes into force;

Sch.7
para.2

(d) *buildings which have not been consecrated but which are licensed for public worship on or after 1st March 1993,* and all articles belonging to them, except in cases where the bishop, after consulting the DAC, directs that the faculty jurisdiction is not to apply. Even where he does give such a direction, the bishop may nevertheless direct that the faculty jurisdiction is to apply for a stated period to one or more specific articles which belong to the building and which he considers, after consulting the DAC, are of outstanding architectural, artistic, historic or archaeological value, or are of a significant monetary value, or are at special risk of being lost or stolen. Orders by the bishop making directions of either kind may be varied or revoked, again after consulting the DAC, and must be registered with the diocesan registrar; it is also recommended that lists containing full details of all the orders made under these provisions and under (c) are kept by the diocesan office and the DAC; and

s.11(2)

s.11(3)

s.11(4) & (5)

s.11(6)
s.28

(e) *books in parochial libraries* within the Parochial Libraries Act 1708[5] (in cases of sale only). Further guidance as to these libraries is given in *A Guide to the Parochial Registers and Records Measure 1978* (see Appendix H).

Sch.7
para.1

In this section of the Code, 'church' includes all the buildings in (a) to (d). It is also important to note that even if works have been recommended in an architect's or surveyor's report under the 1955 Measure, that does not remove the need for a faculty.

139   Even in cases (a) to (d) of the previous paragraph, there are some things (sometimes referred to as 'de minimis') which are of such a minor nature that a faculty is not needed. The chancellor of each diocese must give written guidance about these, after consulting the DAC, and the parish and anyone else who may require a faculty should obtain a copy of that guidance from the diocesan registrar. It *may* cover things such as the following:

s.11(8)

(a)   introduction of cruets, vases, altar linen, authorised service books and hymn books, fire extinguishers, movable hymn boards, and movable bookcases and display stands;

(b)   kneelers and cushions, but not total replacement of hassocks;

(c)   replacement of carpets (in the same material and the same previously authorised colour) and curtains;

(d)   decorative banners used for some strictly temporary displays. (The precise conditions will depend on the chancellor's directions);

(e)   furniture in church halls and furniture, furnishings and minor fixtures in vestries;

(f)   some minor works of routine maintenance, of a kind and up to a maximum cost fixed by the chancellor;

(g)   repairs to paths, repairs to notice boards and repainting them in the same colour, and repairs to pianos using matching materials;

(h)   tuning and adjustment of organs, harmoniums and pianos; and

(i)   inspection and routine maintenance of bells, bell frames, clocks and clock faces.

As will be seen, these should have no material impact on the appearance of the church. However, it has to be stressed that they are merely possible examples, and that the up-to-date official list for the diocese should always be consulted.

140   There are also a few other cases where, exceptionally, a faculty is not required and where what is proposed can be authorised in some other way. These relate to tombstones; monuments and memorials, temporary re-ordering of churches; and emergency demolition, and are dealt with in Section VII of this Code.

Seeking the Advice of the DAC

141   Assuming a faculty is required, the first step towards obtaining it should be to seek the DAC's advice (except in cases which are confined to exhumation or reservation of grave spaces). There is no prescribed form for the request for advice, but the DAC secretary may well be able to supply a non-statutory form, and in that case all those seeking formal advice from the DAC are recommended to use it. In any event, the request should include a list of all the works proposed, giving a summary of each of them, and should be accompanied by all the designs, plans and documents which are necessary to give full details of the proposals; the documents should also be listed. The documents should normally in-   FJR r.3(1)

clude scale drawings giving the plan, elevation and section of the proposed work, together with perspective views, specifications of maker and workshop, and material, colour, size, design and style, and estimates, as appropriate. In some cases, models will also be helpful. The information the DAC is recommended to request includes the name and address of the applicant and on whose behalf the advice is requested; the names of the parish and benefice; details of the parochial church council discussions and voting figures; copies of relevant correspondence and application for grants from English Heritage; and information as to whether the church is in a conservation area and whether the building or structure is listed or of special architectural interest – if so, the grade of the listing should be given. Where practicable those who are applying for the Committee's advice should also submit a draft of the petition form (see para. 149), with as many as possible of the questions answered; the secretary should be prepared to supply blank petition forms for this purpose.

142   Failure to describe the proposals properly or supply all the relevant information may well lead to difficulty or delay, at this stage or later, and it is recommended that in general anyone who has been giving professional advice on the proposals should also be consulted about the terms of the application to the DAC and what material should accompany it. It is also recommended that, where at all possible, duplicate copies of the documents are supplied, so that when the originals are returned to the person or body seeking advice the DAC can retain the duplicates for reference; this may help to avoid delay at a later stage.

143   After any necessary visit (see paras 103 and 117 and Appendix A Part III), and after it has considered the matter, the DAC will issue a certificate in a form prescribed by the Faculty Jurisdiction Rules, recording that it has decided: FJR App.B / Form 1

    (a)   to recommend the proposals, or at least to raise no objection. This may be with or without provisos; or   FJR r.3(2)

    (b)   not to recommend the proposals, giving the main reasons.   FJR r.3(3)

The documents will be returned with the certificate. It is recommended that the Diocesan Advisory Committee secretary stamps or marks them so that they can if necessary be identified later as the documents which the DAC has seen and on which it has based its decision. It is also recommended that the secretary retains the list or a copy of the list of documents. Where duplicates of the documents were supplied as recommended in the previous paragraph, these will be retained by the DAC.   FJR r.3(2)

144 The certificate will contain a description of the proposals. This will form the basis of future documents, and it is recommended that the DAC takes a good deal of care to produce a clear and accurate description which can be understood without reference to any plan, drawing or other document except those which are specifically mentioned. In addition, the person or body which applied for the DAC's advice should check the description carefully; if there appears to be any mistake in it, this should be taken up immediately with the DAC secretary. Another aspect of the certificate is that it states whether, in the DAC's opinion, the proposal will result in a material alteration to the appearance of the church or affect its setting, and this too will normally be important at a later stage; where necessary, the diocesan registrar should be asked to advise on the legal meaning of 'material alteration'. It is also recommended that the DAC gives its view as to whether any part of r.12(3) (see para. 163) applies; in the case of a listed building, this will involve giving a view on whether the proposals are likely to affect its character as a building of special architectural or historic interest. FJR App.B Form 1

145 It is possible to lodge a petition for a faculty even without seeking the DAC's advice, or even if the Committee has decided not to recommend the proposals. However, failing to seek the Committee's advice may well lead to delay, because until the DAC has decided to recommend the proposal or not to oppose it the faculty petition cannot be allocated to the archdeacon, even if the archdeacon would normally have jurisdiction (see para.162). An unfavourable decision by the DAC obviously means that the prospects of obtaining a faculty are greatly reduced, and the matter will again need to go to the chancellor in any event (see para. 162). Because of this, it is generally better to try to reformulate the proposals in a way which the DAC will be able to find more acceptable. FJR r.3(3) & (5)

146 Applications by the archdeacon or chancellor for the DAC's advice, and procedure for dealing with them, are covered in paragraphs 167 and 176.

Lodging the Petition and Register of Petitions

147 The next step is to lodge the petition for a faculty at the diocesan registry, whose address can be found in the Diocesan Year Book or the *Church of England Year Book* or obtained from the diocesan office. At this stage, those who are putting forward the proposal must consider whether it involves total or partial demolition of the church and take the diocesan registrar's advice if there is any element of doubt. The concept of 'partial demolition' or FJR r.5(4)

'demolition of part' of the church is a broad one, although precisely what it covers depends on the facts of each case. If total or partial demolition is involved, it will be necessary not only to comply with the requirements set out in the following paragraphs but also to satisfy those set out in paragraphs 188-195.

148   The next question which arises is who can petition for a faculty. The categories are as follows: s.16(1)

(a)   *the minister and churchwardens* (or, if there is no minister, the churchwardens) are the normal petitioners. The *parochial church council* is quite often joined as a petitioner, and may need to do so in order to give undertakings to the consistory court; s.16(1)(b)

(b)   *the archdeacon* may also petition, for example if he finds that the parish is not taking the necessary steps for the care of the church and attempts to persuade it to do so have failed (see paras 229-231). The 1991 Measure provides for a bishop to appoint a person to act in the archdeacon's place in relation to faculty proceedings if the archdeaconry is vacant, the archdeacon is unable to act because of absence or illness (the Faculty Jurisdiction Rules deal with evidence of incapacity for this purpose), or if the bishop considers that the archdeacon is unable or unwilling to act for some other reason or that it would be inappropriate for him to do so. If the archdeacon or a person appointed by the bishop to act for him commences or intervenes in proceedings for obtaining a faculty (but not an injunction or a restoration order – see paras 224-227), and the bishop approves this beforehand after consulting the Diocesan Board of Finance, the Board is to pay the archdeacon's or other person's costs and expenses, including any which he is required by the court to pay; and s.16(1)(a)

s.16(3)
FJR App.B
Form 12
FJR r.26

s.16(4)

(c)   *it is also possible for any other person to petition who appears to the consistory court to have a sufficient interest.* This includes a parishioner or a person on the church electoral roll; for example, a parishioner will petition if he wishes to obtain a faculty to reserve a grave space or to erect a special tombstone which is outside the scope of the normal authority delegated to the incumbent (see paras 208-209). A parishioner who is a potential donor of an article to the church may petition for a faculty authorising the church to accept it, sometimes with the minister and churchwardens as joint petitioners (see para. 128(a)). In some cases the lay rector has responsibility for the repair of the chancel and will be able to petition on that basis. s.16(1)(c)

s.16(2)

149　The petition must be in the form laid down by the Faculty Jurisdiction Rules, which is reproduced in Appendix C to this Code, with any necessary variations (see para. 183), and a copy of the form will normally be supplied by the DAC secretary if the DAC decides to recommend the proposals or not to oppose them. The petition form is also available from the diocesan registrar; in addition, it is published separately by Church House Publishing and is available from Church House Bookshop, Great Smith Street, London SW1P 3BN.

FJR r.3(4);
App. B
Form 2

150　It is the petitioner's responsibility to see that the form is properly filled in and accompanied by the correct documents; failure to do so is likely to result in delay or difficulty later. In case of doubt, the petitioner should also consult the diocesan registrar at the outset. All the questions must be answered and the proposals must be fully and accurately described; the proper course will be to copy the description in the DAC's certificate. If the proposals have been changed subsequently they should be resubmitted to the DAC before the petition is lodged. The petition must be accompanied by all the plans and other documents needed to give details of what is proposed, and in particular all those referred to in the description, together with a list of documents. In addition to the information given in the petition, the registrar will need to know whether the church is in a conservation area; in the case of work affecting a building or structure other than the church (for example a tomb or monument) the registrar will need to know whether it is separately listed as of special architectural or historic interest and, if so, what its grade is.

151　A fee is payable by the petitioner on lodging the petition (see paras 204-206) (although this is not charged in some dioceses, at least where the parish is asking for the faculty). The precise amount depends on whether the petition is for an archdeacon's or a chancellor's faculty, and if a petition which originally went to the archdeacon subsequently has to be referred to the chancellor a further fee will normally be payable. The petitioners should therefore ask the diocesan registrar to notify them of the correct fee.

152　The DAC secretary is required to keep a register of petitions which have been formally referred to the DAC for advice by the chancellor or the archdeacon. For that purpose, the diocesan registrar must inform the DAC secretary as soon as the registrar receives a petition which will have to be referred to the DAC by or on behalf of the chancellor or archdeacon (see paras 167 and 176), so that the secretary can enter the details in the register. The register must be available for public inspection, by prior appointment, at a place in

s.15(3)

FJRr.10

s.15(3)

the diocese designated by the bishop. However, it should be stressed that the DAC secretary's duty to maintain the register is completely separate from the Committee's function of giving advice. In addition, the diocesan registrar will in practice need to keep a record of all petitions and how they are progressing, both for the registrar's own purposes and in order to answer queries from those with an interest in the matter. This list is not governed by the 1991 Measure or Rules and is not open to public inspection, but the registrar may be willing to make it available to the DAC secretary to assist with the secretary's statutory duties.

General Citation (or Notice)

153   When petitioners who are a minister or churchwardens or both jointly are ready to lodge the petition for a faculty (other than one for exhumation or reservation of a grave space), they must also complete a general citation (that is, notice of the petition to all concerned, offering an opportunity to submit objections) in the form set out in the Faculty Jurisdiction Rules (which gives 21 days for objections). Copies will be available from the DAC secretary or the diocesan registrar. Again, the petitioners are responsible for completing the form correctly, and must describe the proposals in the same way as in the petition; however, they may ask the diocesan registrar for advice, and should do so if the proposals do not fall within those in Appendix A to the Faculty Jurisdiction Rules which the archdeacon can authorise (see para. 162 and Appendix D).

FJR r.5

FJR App.B
Form 3

FJR r.5(2)

154   Where the petitioners are the minister or churchwardens or both jointly, they must send a copy of the citation to the diocesan registry with the petition and must display copies of the citation as follows:

FJR r.5(3)
FJR r.5(4)

(a)   where the petition relates to the parish church or its churchyard, copies of the citation are to be displayed inside the parish church, on a notice board or in some other prominent position, and on a notice board outside the parish church;

(b)   where the petition relates to another church or place of worship or its churchyard, copies of the citation are to be displayed inside and outside the parish church (or churches) as in (a), and also on a notice board or in some other prominent place inside the church or place of worship concerned and on a notice board outside it; and

(c)   copies of the citation must normally be displayed for a continuous period of at least 14 days. This must include at least one Sunday when the church where the citation is displayed is used for worship, and if the church is not normally

68

used for worship on a Sunday one possible course is to hold a special service, possibly a brief one followed by a social event including an explanation of the proposals. The chancellor also has certain general powers to give directions. (Special periods apply in cases of chancellor's faculties within r.12(3) of the Faculty Jurisdiction Rules - see para.163.)

FJR r.31

If there is no notice board within the grounds of the church or place of worship under (a) or (b), the notice which is to be displayed outside that building is to be displayed on the outside of or near to the principal door, and also in some other prominent position readily visible to the public.

155   Where the petitioners are *not* the minister or churchwardens, they should obtain the diocesan registrar's directions as to the citation.

FJR r.5(3)

156   In any case, the registrar may give special directions if he or she considers that:

FJR r.5(5)

(a)   the proposals are not adequately described in the general citation;

(b)   a copy of the citation should be displayed inside or outside some other church or place of worship in the parish, or in some other prominent position in the parish (inside or outside a building) where it will be clearly visible to the public, or both; or

(c)   a copy of the citation should be displayed for longer than the normal period.

(b) or (c) or both will be appropriate where the registrar takes the view that they are desirable in order to give adequate notice of the proposals to all concerned.

157   Where the petition relates solely to exhumation or the reservation of a grave space, or where the chancellor has given directions regarding general citation (see para.171(a)), the registrar is to complete the form of general citation and give appropriate directions as to its display. (In some cases of exhumation, the chancellor may dispense with the general citation – see para. 199).

FJR r.12(8)

158   Once the general citation has been displayed in accordance with the requirements set out above and, where applicable, the requirements under paragraphs 172 and 194(d), the petitioners are to return it to the registrar with the certificate of execution at the end duly completed to confirm where and how it has been displayed. The registrar will normally enquire whether the requirements not covered by the certificate – for example, as to display on a Sunday on which the church is used for worship – have also been satisfied.

FJR r.5(6)

159　The previous paragraphs set out the legal requirements regarding the general citation. However, it is also strongly recommended that notice of the petition is included in the parish magazine or news-sheet (or both) and read out at the principal Sunday services – the legal objection to this under s.4 of the Parish Notices Act 1837 has now been abolished – and that copies of the plans and documents are displayed in the parish hall or some other convenient place, so that all involved with the church will be aware of what is happening and their right to object.

s.24

160　The purpose of citation is to give all those who have a legitimate interest in the proposals an opportunity to object if they wish. Special rules apply where a person or body is 'specially cited' – that is, given notice on an individual basis – as well as to cases of total or partial demolition and to cases where special directions are given (see paras 171-173 and 194). In general, however, the citation will give the period of 21 days from the date when the citation is first displayed to lodge a notice of objection, containing the information required by the form of citation, at the diocesan registry and with the petitioners. The possible categories of objectors are listed in paragraph 178, and that paragraph and paragraph 179 also explain the legal consequences of lodging an objection.

Matters within the Archdeacon's Jurisdiction

161　Before the faculty proceedings can go any further, it is necessary to establish whether the petition falls within the archdeacon's jurisdiction, or whether it has to go to the chancellor for a decision. The former archdeacon's certificate procedure is now abolished, and the archdeacon will be granting faculties with the same legal force and effect as the chancellor's. However, the archdeacon cannot issue injunctions or make restoration orders (see paras 224-227) or grant an interim faculty pending a final decision on a faculty petition. As explained in paragraph 148(b), the 1991 Measure makes provision for the bishop to appoint someone other than the archdeacon to act in the archdeacon's place where necessary.

s.14(1);
FJR r.6

s.16(3)

THE SCOPE OF THE JURISDICTION

162　The first step in giving the archdeacon jurisdiction will be for the chancellor to confer that jurisdiction formally, as the chancellor is required to do under the 1991 Measure. Even then it is open to the archdeacon to decline to exercise the jurisdiction, for example because of special circumstances in the archdeaconry. However, assuming the archdeacon has not done this, the registrar will initially refer a petition for a faculty to the archdeacon if:

s.14(2)
FJR r.7(2)

FJR r.6

(a)   it is confined to matters within Appendix A of the Faculty Jurisdiction Rules (which is reproduced in Appendix D to this Code); and

(b)   it is unopposed; and   s.14(2)&(3)

(c)   the DAC recommends the proposals or raises no objection to them; and

(d)   none of the special cases within r.12(3) of the Faculty Jurisdiction Rules arises (see para. 163).

So far as matters within Appendix A of the Faculty Jurisdiction Rules are concerned, it is important to note that these do not include cases of total or partial demolition (see paras 188-195), which must always be referred to the chancellor.

163   R.12(3) of the Faculty Jurisdiction Rules covers three classes   FJR r.6(1) & 12(3) of case, all of which are particularly sensitive and must, in any event, go to the chancellor for a decision:

(a)   those which involve alteration to or extension of a church which is a listed building to such an extent as is likely to affect its character as a building of special architectural or historic interest;

(b)   those which affect the archaeological importance of the church or archaeological remains existing within the church or its curtilage. (As regards the meaning of 'curtilage' see para. 138(b)); and

(c)   those which involve demolition affecting the exterior of an unlisted church in a conversation area. (Here again, it is considered that 'demolition' includes partial demolition.)

In making the preliminary assessment as to whether a petition falls within any of these categories, the diocesan registrar may well need to obtain guidance from the DAC (see para.144).

164   In addition, a petition must be referred to the chancellor:

(a)   if it is or becomes opposed;   s.14(2) & (3)

(b)   if the archdeacon is the minister of the parish to which   FJR r.7(1) the petition relates, or has been personally involved to such an extent that the archdeacon considers it appropriate to act. (The archdeacon must if practicable inform the diocesan registrar at the outset, and it is recommended that the archdeacon writes to the parish to explain the position and asks them to submit the letter to the registrar with the petition);

(c) if the archdeacon considers that the matter needs to be dealt with as a matter of urgency without reference to the DAC for advice, or may require an injunction or restoration order or an interim faculty, or gives rise to questions of payment of costs and expenses. (All these put the case outside the archdeacon's jurisdiction, so that the archdeacon must inform the registrar of the position.); FJR r.7(3)

(d) if for any reason the archdeacon declines to exercise his jurisdiction over the matter (the archdeacon has a complete discretion here) or declines to grant a faculty (see paras 162 and 169). FJR r.7(2)

s.14(3)(a)

For the precise procedure in these cases, reference should be made to the Faculty Jurisdiction Rules. FJR r.6(5), 7, 9(2) & (3)

165 Finally, the registrar must also refer a petition to the chancellor if he or she considers that: FJR r.9(1)

(a) a confirmatory faculty is required (to regularise action already taken);

(b) the proposals raise a question of law, or a question as to the doctrine, ritual or ceremonial of the Church of England, or affect some person's or body's legal rights;

(c) some person or body may need to be specially cited (see paras 171-173 and 194) – for example, the Commonwealth War Graves Commission. This provision overlaps with r.12(3) cases – see para. 163;

(d) it is not clear whether the proposals fall within the archdeacon's jurisdiction;

(e) the DAC has decided against recommending the proposals and has given a certificate to that effect;

(f) the petition raises matters which may justify an injunction; or

(g) for any other reason it is desirable to refer the petition to the chancellor.

Here again, the detailed procedure is laid down in the Faculty Jurisdiction Rules. FJR r.9(3)

166 If a matter is already being dealt with by the archdeacon, and the registrar becomes aware that the information in the petition is incorrect or incomplete, so that the matter falls outside the archdeacon's jurisdiction, the registrar must notify the archdeacon and refer the case to the chancellor. FJR r.9(2)

167   On the basis that the archdeacon does have jurisdiction to deal with the petition and is willing in principle to exercise it, the archdeacon must seek the advice of the DAC before granting a faculty. However, if the DAC has already issued a certificate within the past twelve months for the same proposals (see .para. 143), it may simply confirm that it does not wish to alter its previous decision. To avoid unnecessary delay, it is recommended that:-

s.15(2);
FJR r.6(3)

(a)   the archdeacons authorise the registrar to approach the DAC automatically on all petitions which fall within the archdeacons' jurisdiction and to ask for the DAC's advice on them on the archdeacon's behalf; and

(b)   the DAC authorises a sub-committee or the secretary to confirm on its behalf that it does not wish to alter the advice in certificates given within the previous twelve months. (It will then be necessary to check the petition and see whether the proposals are in fact the same as those on which the DAC has already advised.)

168   If the archdeacon decides to grant a faculty, this is endorsed on the petition and the petition returned to the registrar. Provided no objection is received within the period of notice for objection, the registrar issues the faculty in the form prescribed by the Rules. This form specifies the period for completing the work and requires a certificate of completion to be sent to the diocesan registry within that period - the registrar will send a blank certificate of completion to the petitioners with the faculty. It is recommended that the registrar notifies the DAC secretary of the grant of the faculty and completion of the work.

FJR r.6(4)

FJR App.B
Forms 5 & 6

169   However, if the archdeacon is not willing to grant a faculty, for whatever reason, that does not conclude the matter, and if the petition is pursued it must be referred back to the registrar for referral to the chancellor.

s.14(3)(a)

Matters within the Chancellor's Jurisdiction

170   All petitions which the archdeacon cannot or does not wish to deal with, or where he decides against granting a faculty, must be referred back to the registrar for referral to the chancellor.

FJR r.11(1)

SPECIAL REQUIREMENTS AS REGARDS NOTICE ETC

171   The main provisions as regards this in the Faculty Jurisdiction Rules are as follows:

(a)   the chancellor may direct notice of the citation to be published in one or more newspapers or other publications, and may direct what form the publication is to take;

FJR r.12(2)

(b)   the chancellor may order any person or body to be 'specially cited', that is, given notice on an individual basis. The person or body specially cited has 28 days from service of the special citation to send notice of objection to the registrar and the petitioners or to send the registrar comments on the proposals;

FJR r.12(1)

FJR r.12(6)

(c)   where proposals for a churchyard will or may affect a grave or memorial maintained by the Commonwealth War Graves Commission (see para. 124), the Commission must be specially cited; and

FJR r.12(5)

(d)   there are special provisions for cases within r.12(3), which are dealt with in the following paragraph.

172   The cases to which r.12(3) apply have already been described in paragraph 163. In all these cases, English Heritage, the local planning authority and the relevant National Amenity Society or Societies must be specially cited unless the chancellor in each case is satisfied that the body concerned has already been notified of the proposals. (The position as regards special citation is the same as under (b) of the previous paragraph.) In addition, the general citation (see paras 153-160) must be displayed in a prominent position outside the church, visible to the general public for 28 days. In cases under (a) or (c) the chancellor must direct that a notice stating the substance of the petition must be published in a newspaper circulating in the locality within the period which he directs or, if no period is specified, within 14 days of the direction. In this or any other case English Heritage may apply in the form and within the time limit fixed by the Rules to give evidence at the hearing, even if it is not a party.

FJR r.12(3)

FJR r.12(4)

FJR r.23
App. B
Form 10

173   Under the Faculty Jurisdiction Rules, where the chancellor considers that the petition relates or may relate to an article or matter of historic or artistic interest (including any ornament, movable object, part of a building or article or anything fixed to the land or a building), notice of the petition and copies of the petition itself and the accompanying documents are to be sent to the Council for the Care of Churches, which may respond within six weeks with a report or an application to give evidence. (This rule is intended in particular to deal with objects of special significance for artistic or historical reasons, but the Council's advice may also be needed

FJR r.14

where the DAC lacks special expertise.) The Council for the Care of Churches may also apply to give evidence in any other case, even though it is not a party; in any case the application must be made in the form and within the time-limit fixed by the Rules.

FJR r.22
App.B Form
10

174   As indicated in the previous two paragraphs, both English Heritage and the Council for the Care of Churches have the right to apply to give evidence in any case, whether or not they fall within any special category, and they do not need to become a party to the proceedings and thus be at risk as to costs (see para. 179) in order to exercise that right.

FJR r.22 &
23

175   Special provisions as regards notice also apply in cases involving total or partial demolition (see para. 194) and exhumation (see para. 199).

ADVICE OF DAC

176   The chancellor must seek the advice of the DAC in all cases except those confined to exhumation or reservation of a grave space or where the chancellor is satisfied that the matter is sufficiently urgent to justify granting a faculty (or issuing an injunction) without the DAC's advice. As in the case of the archdeacon's jurisdiction (see para. 167), if the DAC has already issued a certificate for the same proposals within the past twelve months, it may simply confirm that it does not wish to alter the certificate, and it is recommended that the procedure set out in paragraph 167 for archdeacon's cases is also adopted for those which are to go to the chancellor.

s.15(1);
FJR r.13

177   The Faculty Jurisdiction Commission[6] recommended that if an opposed case was decided against the DAC's advice the chancellor should inform the DAC of the reasons for the decision.

OBJECTIONS TO PETITION

178   Under of the Faculty Jurisdiction Rules any of the following may object to a proposed faculty being granted:

FJR r.15

(a)   a person resident in the parish or entered on the church electoral roll;

(b)   the archdeacon (for whom the same considerations apply as under paragraph 148(b));

(c)   the parochial church council;

(d)   the local planning authority;

(e)   any National Amenity Society; and

(f)   any other body designated by the chancellor in relation to the petition and any other person or body who appears to the chancellor to have a lawful interest in the proposals (for example, a local amenity society).

Such a person or body who wishes to object must send notice of objection to the diocesan registry and the petitioners within the appropriate period (see paras 153, 171-172 and 194). The person or body then becomes a 'party opponent' to the proceedings for all purposes and must supply the registrar and the petitioners with detailed particulars of the objections within 21 days after the registrar directs this to be done.

179   The list of those who can object is, rightly, a long one, so that anyone with legitimate interest may oppose the grant of the faculty, but it is important to note that an objector who becomes a party opponent to the proceedings may become liable for costs; anyone who wishes to avoid this risk should instead apply to give evidence as a judge's witness (see para. 180).

PROCEDURE AND GUIDING PRINCIPLES ON PETITIONS DEALT WITH BY THE CHANCELLOR

180   This Code does not set out to give a comprehensive account of the detailed procedure under the Faculty Jurisdiction Rules or the principles on which the chancellor may act; for this reference should be made to the second edition of *Faculty Jurisdiction of the Church of England* (see Appendix H). However, some aspects of the procedures are mentioned elsewhere in this Section, including the special procedures on demolition, exhumation and reservation of grave spaces (see paras 188-195 and 199-200), and the special position of English Heritage and the Council for the Care of Churches as regards giving evidence (see paras 172-174). Another point of practical importance is that the chancellor has power to call a member of the DAC or the Council for the Care of Churches or *any* other person as a 'judge's witness'. Such a witness can be cross-examined, but can ask questions of the parties with the leave of the chancellor and is not liable for costs. It is open to any person to volunteer or request to give evidence on this basis provided the chancellor agrees; indeed, the Faculty Jurisdiction Commission report[7] recommended that the archdeacon should be prepared to give evidence as a judge's witness about local views which would not otherwise have been voiced. (It is obviously desirable that before fixing the date for the hearing the registrar should give reasonable notice of possible dates to any judge's witness as well as to witnesses for the Council for the Care of Churches and English

FJR r.24

Heritage under paragraphs 172-174 and to the parties themselves, and if possible arrive at a date convenient to all concerned.)

181 So far as guiding principles are concerned, the general principles outlined in paragraphs 3-4 of course apply. As to other relevant principles, it should also be noted by way of example that in considering whether to grant a faculty in a r.12(3) case the chancellor will have regard to the desirability of preserving a listed building or its setting, preserving or enhancing the character or appearance of a conservation area and preserving archaeological remains which are of national importance. Indeed, a recent decision of the Court of Arches[8] has confirmed that in the case of a listed building there is a presumption against allowing a change which would adversely affect its character as of special architectural or historic interest.

182 The form of the faculty in an unopposed case is laid down by the Faculty Jurisdiction Rules. It specifies the time within which the matters which have been authorised are to be completed and requires a certificate of completion to be sent to the diocesan registry within that period – the registrar will supply a blank certificate of completion. The chancellor will give any necessary directions as to the form of the order in an opposed case. It is recommended that the registrar gives notice of the chancellor's decision to all the petitioners and all objectors, to the DAC secretary, to any people or bodies who have been specially cited and have objected to the proposals or sent comments, and to English Heritage or the Council for the Care of Churches in any case where they have applied to give evidence (see paras 171-174). It is also recommended that the registrar notifies the DAC secretary when the work has been completed.

FJR r.11(2)
& App.B
Forms 5 & 6

Forms

183 The Faculty Jurisdiction Rules contain a number of prescribed forms for various stages in the proceedings. These are set out in Appendix B to the Rules and are intended to clarify the issues and to ensure that all concerned have the relevant information. These terms can be obtained from the Rules themselves or the diocesan registry and should in fact be used; attempting to save money by not using the authorised forms is a wasted economy. However, if a form is inappropriate in any respect, it can be adapted as the circumstances require.

FJR r.33(1)

Conditions Attached to Faculties and Deviation from Terms of Faculty

184 A faculty may always be granted subject to conditions, including in particular:

s.12(1)

(a)   conditions requiring the work to be supervised by an archdeacon or some other named person. The person responsible for supervision will need to be given copies of the faculty itself and all accompanying documents. (Where there is no person specifically made responsible for supervising the work, it is recommended that the archdeacon makes a point of checking that the arrangements are satisfactory); or

s.12(i)(a)

(b)   in the case of a faculty authorising disposal of an article, a condition requiring that a stated period must elapse before the disposal takes place, for example to give a museum or art collection an opportunity to acquire it.

s.12(1)(b)

185   Although they are not specifically mentioned in the legislation, other possible conditions include those designed to safeguard wildlife or archaeological remains, or to require prior evaluation, excavation and recording of archaeological remains before the work authorised by the faculty is carried out (see paras 125-127). Conditions may also require work to be completed within a fixed period.

186   If a faculty is granted authorising essential work, the chancellor may order that if the original petitioner does not carry out the work the archdeacon is to be authorised to do so and can recover the cost of carrying out the work from the petitioner.

s.12(2)

187   If after a faculty is granted it is necessary to deviate from the work which the faculty has authorised, or a condition cannot be fully carried out, it is essential to go back to the consistory court for a variation of the terms of the faculty. (The order granting the faculty frequently gives the petitioner 'liberty to apply' to the chancellor if necessary.)

Special Cases

DEMOLITION OR PARTIAL DEMOLITION OF CHURCHES

188   The total or partial demolition of a church (including any other building of the kinds described in paragraph 138) may take place only if it is authorised by:

(a)   *a scheme under the Pastoral Measure 1983* (which applies only to consecrated churches and chapels, and to buildings for use for worship and for church hall purposes which have been consecrated or partly consecrated);[9] or

(b)   *a faculty* (As will be seen from the following paragraphs, both the law and the procedure on an application for a faculty for total or partial demolition of a church differ from the normal provisions); or

(c)   in very exceptional circumstances, under the *special procedure for emergency demolition* outlined in paragraphs 213-216.

189   This is a highly sensitive area, and it is essential that the letter and spirit of the legal requirements are observed. 'Demolition' is not defined, and while it is usually clear whether what is proposed involves total demolition of a church, 'partial demolition' and 'demolition of part' are broad terms. Whether a particular proposal falls within them depends on all the circumstances, and in any case of doubt the diocesan registrar should always be consulted, particularly if what is proposed would have a major impact on the fabric of the church (although lesser works may also amount to 'partial demolition').

190   The procedure under the Pastoral Measure 1983 will always be needed where the site or part of the site of a consecrated church or other consecrated building is to be sold or if for any other reason the legal effects of consecration (in particular the fact that the property is subject to the jurisdiction of the consistory court) are to be removed. Here again, the parish will need to consult the diocesan registrar about the appropriate procedure at an early stage. In addition, the procedure under the Pastoral Measure may, depending on the circumstances, be advisable in the case of a church which is a listed building or in a conservation area in order to test whether the demolition of the building or the relevant part of it might be avoided by finding a suitable alternative use or (exceptionally) by vesting it in the Redundant Churches Fund; whether this solution would meet the need which led to the proposal for demolition has of course to be considered in the light of the particular facts.

191   In almost all cases of faculty petitions for total or partial demolition, the procedure requires the bishop's written consent. (The exception is the 'alternative procedure' available in a very limited range of cases which is explained in paragraph 195.) It is recommended that before giving that consent the bishop considers whether the faculty procedure or the procedure under the Pastoral Measure 1983 would be the more appropriate one in the particular case, and that to assist him in deciding this those who are putting forward the proposals should see that he is provided with the advice of the DAC and the Church Commissioners. If that is not done, it is recommended that the bishop arranges for the diocesan registrar to obtain the appropriate advice on his behalf.   s.17(4)(a)

192   Quite apart from this, the process under the faculty jurisdiction is an elaborate one. Faculty cases involving total or partial demolition must always go to the chancellor, who may not grant the faculty except on one or more of the following grounds: FJR App.A

(a) that the chancellor is satisfied that another church or part
of a church will be erected on the site or curtilage of the
demolished church or part of a church, to take its place;

s.17(2)

(b) in the case of demolition of part of a church, that the
chancellor is satisfied that the part left standing will be used
for public worship of the Church of England for a substantial
period; or

s.17(3)(a)

(c) in the case of demolition of part of a church, that the
chancellor is satisfied that this is necessary for purposes of
repair or alteration of the church, or reconstruction of the part
to be demolished.

s.17(3)(b)

Where the church is a listed building or in a conservation area, the
case will be subject to special requirements which are set out in
paragraph 194(c), and if total demolition is involved listed building
consent or conservation area consent, as appropriate, will also be
needed. (As regards the need for listed building consent or conservation area consent in relation to buildings and structures within the
curtilage of a church, see para. 132(b)).

s.17(5) & (6)
s.31(6)

193 Turning to procedure, the petition must be in the usual form
and provide the usual information so far as relevant, but must also
state on which of the grounds in the previous paragraph the petitioners rely. It must give full details of those grounds and the
circumstances of the case, the details of the arrangements proposed
to meet the situation when the whole or part of the church is
demolished (including disposal of fittings and contents), and information on any other matters on which the court should be informed;
it is essential that the court arrives at a decision with full knowledge
of the circumstances.

FJR r.4

194 As regards notice of the petition:

(a) the petitioners must publish a notice setting out of the
substance of the petition in the London Gazette not more than
four weeks after the petition is lodged at the diocesan registry,
and also in one or more newspapers circulating locally and
any other newspapers directed by the chancellor. The chancellor may fix the period within which the notice must be
inserted in each newspaper other than the London Gazette,
but if not it must be inserted within 14 days after the chancellor
names the newspaper;

s.17(4)(a);
s.17(6)(b);
FJR
r.12(7)(b)

(b) the registrar must give written notice of the petition to
the Council for the Care of Churches and the DAC and allow

s.17(4)(b);
s.17(6)(b);

them 28 days to give advice or send in notice of objection. The chancellor must also consider any advice which the DAC offers to him. In addition, if a member or representative of the Council for the Care of Churches, or anyone else who is not merely being frivolous or vexatious, applies to the chancellor in the prescribed form and within the prescribed time limit laid down by the Faculty Jurisdiction Rules to give evidence in open court, the chancellor must hear that evidence. Thus, for example, an interested parishioner or representative of an amenity society can insist on a hearing and on giving relevant evidence without incurring any risk as regards cost; *(FJR r.12(7)(a); s.17(4)(c); s.17(4)(d); s.17(6)(b); FJR r.21; FJR App.B Forms 10 &11)*

(c)   if the church is a listed building or in a conservation area, the registrar must give written notice of the petition to the Secretary of State, the local planning authority, English Heritage and the National Amenity Societies, giving them 28 days to offer advice or send in notice of objection, and the chancellor must consider any advice offered by any of them. *(s.17(5)(a); s.17(6)(b); FJR r.12(7)(a))* The registrar must also give written notice of the petition to the Royal Commission on the Historical Monuments of England, and members or officers of the Commission must have reasonable access to the church for at least a month in order to record it unless the Commission have stated in writing that they do not wish to do so or have completed the recording; and *(s.17(5)(b); s.17(6)(b))*

(d)   in cases where r.12(3) applies (see paras 163 and 172) the requirements of that rule must also be complied with, except so far as they are already covered by earlier parts of this paragraph. In particular, the general citation must be displayed in a prominent position outside the church visible to the general public for 28 days (see para. 172). *(FJR r.12(4)(a))*

195   Finally, in cases under paragraph 192(c) where partial demolition is needed for the purpose of repair, alteration or reconstruction, there is an alternative to the requirements set out in paragraphs 191 and 194(a)-(c). This applies if the chancellor is satisfied, after consultation with the DAC, that when the repair, alteration or reconstruction is completed the demolition 'will not materially affect' the church's internal or external appearance or architectural, archaeological, artistic or historic character. It is recommended that the chancellor also consults the Council for the Care of Churches where necessary. It is also important to note that in these cases it is still necessary to comply with paragraph 193 and with the special requirements for r.12(3) cases where r.12(3) applies (see paras 172 and 194(d)). *(s.17(6)(a))*

196   The arrangements by which the chancellor normally delegates authority to the incumbent to authorise the erection of tombstones complying with certain conditions are explained in Section VII (paras 208-209).

197   In considering the faculty jurisdiction in relation to churchyards, the questions of wildlife and of archaeological remains (see paras 125-127) will need particularly careful consideration.

198   In addition, the Faculty Jurisdiction Commission Report recommended that:

> (a)   a petitioner for the installation of a private monument should normally be required to make a down payment for its future maintenance as a condition of granting a faculty;[10] and

> (b)   the chancellor when dealing with the re-ordering of a churchyard should obtain specialist advice to safeguard historic, artistic and genealogical interests.[11]

199   Exhumation is a specialist subject outside the scope of this Code, and the diocesan registrar should be consulted at an early stage if exhumation may be required. The Faculty Jurisdiction Rules contain a special provision that in such cases: FJR r.12(9)

> (a)   if the chancellor is satisfied that all the deceased person's near relatives who are still alive (if there are any), and anyone else whom the chancellor thinks it reasonable to regard as concerned in the matter, are petitioners or consent, the chancellor may dispense with the need for citation and grant a faculty at once; and

> (b)   in any other case, the chancellor may dispense with a general citation and direct that the people under (a) who are not petitioners are specially cited.

200   Reservations of grave spaces, and exhumation cases where there is a general citation, are subject to special provisions so far as the general citation is concerned, and it is not necessary to obtain advice from the DAC where those are the only matters involved.   FJR r.12(8)

s.15(1) & (2)

CONTENTS OF CHURCHES

201   As regards contents of churches, deposit of articles in diocesan depositories has already been dealt with in paragraphs 64-65. The Faculty Jurisdiction Commission Report also contained a number

of recommendations on this subject which are of practical importance and are set out in Appendix E to this Code.

Appeals

202   The 1991 Measure does not change the basic system of
faculty appeals laid down by the Ecclesiastical Jurisdiction
Measure 1963.[12] In cases which do not involve matters of 'doctrine,
ritual or ceremonial' any party may appeal to the Court of Arches
(for the province of Canterbury) or the Chancery Court of York (for
the province of York). From there a final appeal lies to the Privy
Council (although that right of final appeal has not been exercised
since the 1963 Measure came into force). In faculty cases which the
chancellor certifies as involving matters of 'doctrine, ritual or
ceremonial' the appeal lies to the Court of Ecclesiastical Causes
Reserved, which has sat only twice since 1963; the only form of
appeal from that court is a petition to Her Majesty to review the
court's findings, and that right of appeal has again not been exercised since the commencement of the 1963 Measure.[13]

203   However, a number of changes have been made by the 1991
Measure in order to rationalise the appeals system:

(a)   appeals to the Court of Arches or the Chancery Court of
York in faculty matters were previously dealt with by the Dean
of the Arches and Auditor (a senior ecclesiastical judge)
sitting alone. Under the 1991 Measure, the Dean will be joined
by two diocesan chancellors designated by him for the purpose of the case, because it is considered more appropriate for
appeals from the chancellor to be heard by a three-person
rather than a one-person court;

Sch.4 paras 3 & 8

(b)   the Court of Arches and Chancery Court of York will
also have jurisdiction to hear appeals from injunctions or
restoration orders made by the chancellor. In addition, they
will hear appeals from the chancellor on preliminary matters,
normally involving procedure, even if the case involved questions of doctrine, ritual or ceremonial. However, no appeal is
to lie to the Court of Arches or the Chancery Court of York in
a faculty matter without the leave of the chancellor or, if the
chancellor refuses, the leave of the Dean of the Arches and
Auditor; the object of this is to prevent the court having to
spend time considering appeals without any substance; and

Sch.4, para.6(a)

Sch.4, para.6(b)

(c)   if the Court of Ecclesiastical Causes Reserved is dealing
with a faculty appeal and finds that it does not in fact involve
any question of doctrine, ritual or ceremonial, it can refer the

Sch.4 para.7

case to the Court of Arches or the Chancery Court of York. Similarly, if it has dealt with the question of doctrine, ritual or ceremonial, but finds that the appeal involves other issues which it does not consider it should deal with itself, it may refer these remaining issues to the Court of Arches or the Chancery Court of York. Conversely, if the Court of Arches or the Chancery Court of York finds that a faculty appeal with which it is dealing involves a question of doctrine, ritual or ceremonial, it may refer the appeal to the Court of Ecclesiastical Causes Reserved. The object is to make sure that the issues on a faculty appeal are in fact dealt with by the appropriate court.

Fees

204   At present, the legal position as regards the diocesan registrar's and chancellor's remuneration for the faculty work is that they are paid by means of fees fixed by Fees Orders by the Fees Advisory Commission of the General Synod under the Ecclesiastical Fees Measure 1986[14] and approved by the Synod itself. The fees are normally reviewed annually, and the main table of faculty fees which will come into force on 1st March 1993 is reproduced in Appendix F to this Code. As the main fees which are payable on lodging the petition are payable by the petitioner, this means that in the majority of faculty cases the initial cost of the system in theory falls on the individual parishes which need to obtain faculties.

205   However, in practice most chancellors have surrendered the majority of their fees (apart from those for hearings before the consistory court dealing with cases on written representations and preparing judgements) on an informal basis in return for annual fees. (In fact, some chancellors do not charge any fees at all.) Similarly, many diocese now pay the diocesan registrar for his faculty work, frequently leaving the parishes to pay nothing directly, and this is obviously an incentive to parishes to comply with ecclesiastical law and to petition for a faculty where one is needed. The Faculty Jurisdiction Commission Report[15] recommended wider use of such arrangements, so that specific fees would only be payable in a limited range of special cases (such as petitions for reservation of grave spaces and faculties to regularise action already taken unlawfully without them) and for hearings (unless the chancellor considered the hearing fee should be waived). Where fees were payable, the Faculty Jurisdiction Commission considered that they should be paid to the Diocesan Board of Finance, which should in turn remunerate the chancellor or registrar; the effect of this

would be, in general, to spread the cost of the faculty system among the parishes as a whole, through the common fund, parish share or quota.

206   The 1991 Measure has made a number of amendments to the   s.10; Sch.6
Ecclesiastical Fees Measure 1986 which would put the Fees Advisory Commission in a position to implement these recommendations, subject to approval by the General Synod. The Fees Advisory Commission has already begun considering this possibility, and plans to continue doing so in 1993.

Notes

1.   s.18

2.   Faculty Jurisdiction Measure 1964 s.7.

3.   6th edition p. A19.

4.   Faculty Jurisdiction Measure 1964 s.6, as amended by the 1991 Measure.

5.   Faculty Jurisdiction Measure 1964 s.4 as amended by the 1991 Measure. Further information about this is to be found in the revised edition of *A Guide to the Parochial Registers and Records Measure 1978* (see Appendix H).

6.   para. 203.

7.   para. 198.

8.   Re All Saints, Melbourne (1992).

9.   Pastoral Measure 1983 s.87(1).

10.   para. 338.

11.   para. 314.

12.   Ecclesiastical Jurisdiction Measure 1963 s.7 & 8.

13.   Ecclesiastical Jurisdiction Measure 1963 s.10 & 11.

14.   s.6.

15.   paras 246-247.

VII SPECIAL CASES –
ALTERNATIVES TO FACULTIES

Introduction

207   There are three types of case where a faculty would normally
be needed, but where an alternative is made available under the
1991 Measure or the Faculty Jurisdiction Rules. These relate to (i)
temporary re-ordering of a church; (ii) emergency demolition of a
church; and (iii) the removal of the legal effects of consecration; the
second and third of these in particular are very much exceptional
procedures, and all of them are to be used only after careful
consideration. However, this Section of the Code opens with a
completely different kind of alternative to a faculty which is not an
exceptional procedure but, on the contrary, the normal method of
authorising the erection of new tombstones, monuments and memorials in churchyards.

Tombstones, Monuments and Memorials

208   The practice varies from one diocese to another, but it is now
normal for the chancellor to delegate authority to the incumbent to
allow the erection in the churchyard of tombstones, monuments and
memorials which comply with a number of conditions laid down in
the delegation. During a vacancy in the benefice, the authority may
be delegated to a team vicar or the priest in charge, or to the rural
dean. In some dioceses, a wider discretion is also delegated to the
archdeacon. Thus a faculty is not required unless what is proposed
falls outside the scope of the delegated authority – which does not
necessarily mean it is objectionable, but means that a faculty
petition will be required so that the proposal can be properly
considered.

209   There is no national code for delegations of this kind, although helpful suggestions appear in *The Churchyards Handbook*

and *The Faculty Jurisdiction of the Church of England* (see Appendix H). The precise terms of the delegation in each diocese (sometimes known as 'Churchyard Regulations') are a matter for the chancellor, although it is recommended that the chancellor consults the DAC about them. The Faculty Jurisdiction Commission report[1] recommended that the regulations or a notice relating to them should be hung up in the church porch, so that those responsible for burials would have an opportunity to find out what the requirements were before making a choice of tombstone; it is also important that all incumbents and all local funeral directors and monumental masons should be familiar with what the chancellor has and has not included in the delegated authority.

Temporary Re-ordering

210   Under the Faculty Jurisdiction Rules, the archdeacon may authorise a scheme of temporary re-ordering of a church by licence (as opposed to a faculty) for a period of not more than twelve months. The application for the licence must be made by the minister and a majority of the parochial church council, and a licence may be granted only if the archdeacon is satisfied that: FJR r.8(1)

> (a)   the scheme does not involve any interference with the fabric of the church;

> (b)   it does not involve fixing anything to the fabric or the disposal of any fixtures; and

> (c)   if it involves moving any item, this will be carried out by a suitably competent or qualified person, the item will be safeguarded and stored in the church or some other place approved by the archdeacon, and it can easily be reinstated.

The Legal Advisory Commission of the General Synod has taken the view that 'disposal' in (b) does not apply to cases where a fixture is *merely* moved from its original position, but that would be covered by (c).

211   The licence may be subject to other conditions. It may not be extended for a further period, so that it is essential to petition for a faculty if the re-ordering is to continue. However, if those concerned do petition for a chancellor's faculty not less than two months before the licence is due to expire, the licence will continue automatically until the chancellor reaches a decision on the petition. Copies of the licence must be sent to the diocesan registrar and the DAC secretary. If the archdeacon is not willing to grant the licence, for whatever reason, he is to advise the minister that it is open to him   FJR r.8(2) - (5)

to apply to the chancellor for an interim faculty authorising the scheme.

212 The object of these provisions is to allow a parish a limited and carefully-controlled opportunity to discover whether a particular scheme of re-ordering meets its needs before petitioning for a faculty to authorise such a scheme. It is recommended that the archdeacon takes the following into account in exercising his discretion:

(a) the DAC should be consulted;

(b) the archdeacon should of course satisfy himself that the changes will be easily and completely reversible at the end of the twelve month period if the parish does not apply for a faculty or a faculty is not granted. To a large extent this is covered by the conditions in paragraph 210);

(c) the archdeacon should have regard to any significant minority on the parochial church council or any significant body of opinion in the parish as a whole which is against the proposal; where this exists, he should consider whether it would be more appropriate for the matter to go to the chancellor at the outset, so that all those opposed to the re-ordering have an opportunity to state their objections formally in court. On the other hand, the archdeacon should also bear in mind that the fact that the parochial church council was not unanimous in favour of the scheme is not in itself a ground for refusing a licence. There is almost certain to be some hesitation about a proposed re-ordering, and an experiment for a temporary period will normally be the only way of testing it in practice and discovering whether it is in fact a satisfactory and generally acceptable arrangement; and

(d) any licence which is issued should be in writing, in the form laid down by the Faculty Jurisdiction Rules, and copies should be sent to the diocesan registrar and the DAC secretary.

FJR App.B
Form 7
FJR r.8(3)

Emergency Demolition (Total or Partial)

213 Under the 1991 Measure, the chancellor has power to authorise total or partial demolition of a church in writing, without going through the faculty procedure, where:

s.18

(a) demolition is necessary in the interests of safety or health or (in partial demolition cases) for the preservation of the church, and in view of the urgency of the matter there is not sufficient time to obtain a faculty; and

s.18(1)(a)

(b)   if the church is a listed building or in a conservation area, it is not practicable to secure safety or health, or the preservation of the building, by repairs or works providing temporary support or shelter, and the proposed demolition is limited to the minimum which is immediately necessary.   s.18(1)(b)

As regards the meaning of 'partial demolition', see paragraph 189.

214   As has already been stated, this is a highly exceptional procedure, and the requirements set out in the previous paragraph will be strictly observed. It is recommended that if time allows the Church Commissioners are consulted about proposals affecting a consecrated building (compare paras 190-191). In the case of partial demolition of a church which is a listed building or a building in a conservation area, the person to whom the authorisation is issued must in any event notify the local planning authority of what the works were as soon as practicable after they have been carried out. However, it is strongly recommended that the persons concerned consult the local planning authority before the demolition if at all possible; this will enable the authority's professional officers to advise and will reduce the risk of questions arising later as to whether the demolition was really necessary. In the case of total demolition of a church which is a listed building or a building in a conservation area, the local planning authority of course have to be brought in because of the need for listed building consent or conservation area consent (see para. 132). (As regards the position of buildings and structures within the curtilage of a church, see para. 132(b)). Whether or not a listed building or conservation area is involved, the 1991 Measure requires copies of the chancellor's authorisation under the section to be sent to the local planning authority and the Council for the Care of Churches.   s.18(2)(b)

s.18(3)

215   In addition, the authorisation may require the person to whom it is issued to carry out specified restoration work afterwards (subject to obtaining any necessary faculty).   s.18(2)(a)

216   It is recommended that those applying should, if practicable, be the minister and churchwardens, and if time allows the parochial church council, and that they should begin by attempting to contact the diocesan registrar if possible, unless the emergency is so pressing that they have no alternative but to go at once to the chancellor direct. The evidence they have available will vary with the circumstances of the particular case – for example, they may well need to show that their application has the support of the church's architect or surveyor – but they must make out a clear case for using the chancellor's exceptional powers.

Removal of Legal Effects of Consecration

217   The Faculty Jurisdiction Commission received evidence that there were some consecrated buildings on property not owned by the Church of England – particularly cemetery chapels in local authority cemeteries – which were no longer used for their original purpose but had simply been allowed to fall into disrepair, in particular because of uncertainty as to whether they could be repaired, altered or demolished without a faculty.

218   The 1991 Measure attempts to tackle this problem by making it possible, in very restricted circumstances, for the bishop to remove the legal effects of consecration from the property, so that it can be repaired or altered without a faculty or disposed of. What the section does is to provide that where the archdeacon finds that a consecrated building or land is *not* held or controlled by one of the Church of England bodies which normally hold consecrated property (for example, an incumbent) or by the Diocesan Board of Finance, and that no purpose will be served by its remaining subject to the legal effects of consecration, he may apply to the bishop for an order removing those legal effects, including any further control under the faculty system. The new power is not available for normal Church property; it provides a procedure for removing the legal effects of consecration from buildings or land which are not in ecclesiastical ownership in cases where the procedure under the Pastoral Measure 1983 is not possible or really appropriate. `s.22(1)`

219   The bishop's order may impose conditions or requirements as to: `s.22(2)`

(a)   the preservation or disposal of any human remains which are believed to be buried in or under the building or in the land concerned, and any tombstones, monuments or memorials commemorating the deceased persons. These conditions or requirements need the consent of the Home Office, and may apply or adapt the provisions on such matters in the Pastoral Measure 1983; and `s.22(2)(a)` `s.22(3)`

(b)   maintaining orderly behaviour (bearing in mind that, in a spiritual as opposed to a legal sense, the place retains its consecrated character). `s.22(2)(b)`

There are also detailed provisions as regards the enforcement of the conditions or requirements. `s.22(5)-(8)`

220   The following points also need to be borne in mind in considering the use of the new procedure:

(a) there is no legal requirement to obtain the consent of the owner of the building or land (subject to special provisions regarding Crown land), but the diocesan registrar will need to know who does own the land in order to be satisfied that the technical requirements as regards ownership are satisfied and to judge whether some other procedure would be more appropriate. In any case, it is obviously important to consult the owner if at all possible, in particular on whether the legal effects of consecration still serve a useful purpose, before the archdeacon initiates the procedure;

s.23

(b) enquiries should also be made about the possible existence of any burials, tombstones, monuments or memorials, so that suitable conditions can be imposed after consultation with the Home Office and containing its consent. In all cases where there are or may be burials, tombstones, monuments or memorials, the Commonwealth War Graves Commission should also be consulted (see para. 124);

(c) it is normally also desirable to consult the minister and parochial church council at the parish, and ask them to 'keep an eye' on the property afterwards, especially if any conditions or requirements have been imposed, so that breaches can be brought to the archdeacon's notice without delay; and

(d) if conditions or requirements have been imposed, the diocesan registrar will need to be asked to register them as a local land charge, and should also be consulted immediately if there is a breach, so that the registrar can advise on the appropriate enforcement action.

s.22(8)

Notes

1.   *The Continuing Care of Churches and Cathedrals,* para. 313.

VIII ENFORCEMENT

Introduction

221   Some aspects of this subject have already been discussed in earlier Sections - for example, the archdeacon's power to order the removal of an article to a place of safety (see paras 66-70), intervention by the archdeacon in faculty proceedings (see paras 148(b) and 178(b)) and cases where the chancellor authorises the archdeacon to carry out work permitted by a faculty if the person who petitioned for the faculty fails to do so (see para. 186). However, this final Section of this Code deals with two other aspects of the subject – the new powers given to the chancellor to take action over defaults, and the archdeacon's power to summon an extraordinary meeting of the parochial church council or an extraordinary parochial church meeting to discuss defaults. These new powers emphasise the responsibilities laid on ministers, churchwardens and parochial church councils by the new legislation, and the importance of their understanding and fulfilling their legal duties.

The Chancellor's Powers

222   The 1991 Measure gives the chancellor important powers to enforce the law relating to churches, churchyards and articles belonging to them. The basic provisions on this new aspect of the chancellor's jurisdiction – which give new 'teeth' to the law on faculties – fall into four parts: s.13

    (a)   power to order a party to faculty proceedings whose act or default led to the proceedings to pay the resulting costs and expenses;

(b)   power to issue an injunction to restrain an unlawful act;

(c)   power to make a restoration order requiring the position to be restored as far as possible to what it was before an unlawful act was committed; and

(d)   provisions as regards contempt of court.

PAYMENT OF COSTS AND EXPENSES

223   Under the 1991 Measure, where one person has petitioned for a faculty, and the chancellor considers another person who is a party to the proceedings was wholly or partly responsible for an act or default which led to the proceedings (for example, because that person carried out work in the church without the necessary faculty, and the minister and churchwardens are now applying for a faculty to regularise the situation), the chancellor may order that other person to pay the whole or part of any resulting costs and expenses, including the cost of any work authorised by the faculty, so far as they have been caused by that person's conduct. If the chancellor finds that the person responsible is not already a party to the faculty proceedings, the chancellor may add that person as a party so that the jurisdiction to order payment of costs and expenses can be exercised against him (although this procedure is intended only for exceptional circumstances). However, an order for payment cannot be made in respect of acts committed six years or more before the proceedings began, subject to certain special provisions where the facts have been deliberately concealed.

s.13(1)

s.13(2) & (3)

s.13(7), (9) & (10)

INJUNCTIONS

224   Where it appears to the chancellor at any time, whether or not any faculty proceedings about the matter are in progress, that a person intends to commit or continue committing, or to cause or allow someone else to commit, an act in relation to the church, the churchyard or an article belonging to the church which is contrary to ecclesiastical law (for example, doing work to the church without the necessary faculty), the 1991 Measure provides that the chancellor may issue an injunction restraining that person from that course of conduct.

s.13(4)

225   The procedure for these cases is dealt with in the Measure itself and the Enforcement Rules. An application for an injunction may be made by the archdeacon or by anyone else who appears to the chancellor or the registrar to have a sufficient interest in the matter – this might, for example, include English Heritage, the local planning authority or a National Amenity Society – and the

s.13(6);
ER r.3-8

Rules lay down the form of application and the supporting affidavit evidence which is required and on whom the application is to be served, as well as containing further provisions on evidence and the hearing. In addition, the rules provide for the possibility of an emergency application where there is not time to comply with the normal formalities, and with cases where chancellors consider it necessary as a result of information which they have received to issue an injunction without an archdeacon or anyone else making an application for one. It is necessary to seek the DAC's advice before issuing the injunction unless the chancellor is satisfied that the matter is sufficiently urgent to act without that advice. In cases where the archdeacon applies for an injunction (or a restoration order – see paras 226-227), it is recommended that, where practicable, the archdeacon obtains a promise of financial support from the Diocesan Board of Finance before the application is made (see para. 148(b)).   s.15(1)

RESTORATION ORDERS

226   Under the 1991 Measure, where it appears to the chancellor at any time, whether or not any faculty proceedings about the matter are in progress, that a person has already committed an act contrary to ecclesiastical law in relation to the church, the churchyard or an article belonging to the church, or has already caused or allowed someone else to do so, the chancellor may make a restoration order requiring that person to take stated steps within a stated time to restore the position as far as possible to what it was immediately before the unlawful act. Here again, the order may not be made on the basis of an act committed six years or more ago, subject to special provisions for cases where the facts have been deliberately concealed.   s.13(5)

s.13(8)-(10)

227   The procedure is basically the same as for injunctions, and is regulated by the same rules (see para. 225). The main exception is that where the chancellor is contemplating making a restoration order even though no one has applied for one, the chancellor should first consider whether it would be desirable to require the person concerned to attend the court and hear what that person has to say on whether or not the order should be made.   ER r.9

CONTEMPT

228   Finally, the real sanction for disobedience to a special citation, injunction or restoration order is that failure to comply with any of these orders without reasonable cause is made a contempt of court and can be punished on that basis. The 1991 Measure also includes a new general provision about contempt of the ecclesias-   s.13(11)

Sch.4 para.11

tical courts, under which the ecclesiastical court may refer to the High Court a case where it is alleged that there has been a contempt of the ecclesiastical court. The High Court has power to enquire into the allegation, hear any witnesses and statements in defence and, if the contempt is proved, deal with the person in the same ways as a person guilty of a contempt of the High Court itself.

Archdeacon's Power to Convene Meetings to Discuss Defaults

229   Although the chancellor is given much increased powers to deal with breaches of ecclesiastical law, the 1991 Measure recognises that so far as breaches of the faculty requirements and failure to take action which is needed for the care of the church or its contents are concerned, it is better if possible to resolve the matter pastorally, without legal proceedings. The Measure therefore provides that if the archdeacon considers that: s.20

>   (a)   something has been done in the parish which should not have been done without a faculty; or

>   (b)   there has been a failure to take action which should have been taken in connection with the care of the church or an article belonging to it;

he may convene an extraordinary parochial church council meeting, or an extraordinary parochial church meeting of those on the church electoral roll, in order to discuss the matter. The archdeacon will then either take the chair or appoint someone else to act as chairman. Subject to the provisions of the 1991 Measure, the procedure will be regulated by the Church Representation Rules.

230   Before taking action under this provision, the archdeacon will of course have held informal talks with the minister and church-wardens; assuming these have failed to resolve the problem, it may well be desirable for the archdeacon to use the power to take the chair at the extraordinary meeting. It may also be desirable for the archdeacon to be accompanied by the chairman or another representative of the DAC and, depending on the nature of the problem, by the diocesan registrar or diocesan secretary or the rural dean. The representative of the DAC, for example, will be able to help the archdeacon in emphasising that the proceedings, far from being arbitrary, are part of a carefully considered system, and in explaining precisely why it is so important to comply with the legal requirements.

231   The outcome of the meeting will normally be a request by the archdeacon for confirmation, preferably within a stated time-scale,

that the work which the meeting agreed should be done, or any other action (for example, applying for a confirmatory faculty) which was agreed upon, has in fact been carried out. In appropriate cases the archdeacon should not hesitate to invoke the chancellor's jurisdiction if all else fails, and for that purpose it is important to have an independent note of the proceedings at the extraordinary meeting. However, archdeacons will of course make every effort to resolve problems of this kind themselves on a pastoral basis, and it may well be that by explaining the legal requirements to the parish and having a frank discussion of the practical aspects of complying with them, including any financial problems, the archdeacon will not only help to overcome the immediate difficulty but will leave the parish in a better position to fulfil its legal obligations in the future.

APPENDIX A

PART I

FUNCTIONS OF DIOCESAN ADVISORY COMMITTEES PRESCRIBED BY SCHEDULE 2 TO THE 1991 MEASURE

1. The functions of a Diocesan Advisory Committee shall be –

(a) to act as an advisory body on matters affecting places of worship in the diocese and, in particular, to give advice when requested by any of the persons specified in paragraph 2 below on matters relating to -

(i) the grant of faculties;

(ii) the architecture, archaeology, art and history of places of worship;

(iii) the use, care, planning, design and redundancy of places of worship;

(iv) the use and care of the contents of such places;

(v) the use and care of churchyards and burial grounds;

(b) to review and assess the degree of risk to materials, or of loss to archaeological or historic remains or records, arising from any proposals relating to the conservation, repair or alteration of places of worship, churchyards and burial grounds and the contents of such places;

(c) to develop and maintain a repository of records relating to the conservation, repair and alteration of places of worship, churchyards and burial grounds and other material (including inspection reports, inventories, technical information and photographs) relating to the work of the committee;

(d) to issue guidance for the preparation and storage of such records;

(e) to make recommendations as to the circumstances when the preparation of such a record should be made a condition of a faculty;

(f) to take action to encourage the care and appreciation of places of worship, churchyards and burial grounds and the contents of such places, and for that purpose to publicise methods of conservation, repair, construction, adaptation and re-development;

(g) to perform such other functions as may be assigned to the committee by any enactment, by any Canon of the Church of England or by resolution of the diocesan synod or as the committee may be requested to perform by the bishop or chancellor of the diocese.

2. The persons referred to in paragraph 1(a) above are–

(a) the bishop of the diocese;

(b) the chancellor of the diocese;

(c) the archdeacons of the diocese;

(d) the parochial church councils in the diocese;

(e) intending applicants for faculties in the diocese;

(f) the pastoral committee of the diocese;

(g) persons engaged in the planning, design or building of new places of worship in the diocese, not being places within the jurisdiction of the consistory court;

(h) such other persons as the committee may consider appropriate.

PART II

OTHER FUNCTIONS SUGGESTED BY THE FACULTY JURISDICTION COMMISSION

These functions are suggested in Appendix 5 to the Faculty Jurisdiction Commission Report *The Continuing Care of Churches and Cathedrals*, and under paragraph 1(g) of Schedule 2 to the 1991 Measure (see Part I of this Appendix) all or any of them may be assigned to the DAC of a particular diocese by resolution of the diocesan synod or by means of a request from the bishop or the chancellor to perform them. (However, it is considered that even if this is not done the DAC's Schedule 2 functions would cover a large proportion of what is set out below).

(a) To disseminate information as to the works and other matters for which a faculty is required.

(b) To develop and maintain a library relating to the work of the committee.

(c) To keep in touch with the Council for the Care of Churches and other official bodies of the Church of England within the diocese or elsewhere, and with official bodies of other Churches, government departments, other public bodies, local authorities and amenity societies so far as they are concerned with aspects of the committee's work.

(d)   To conduct discussions and negotiations on behalf of the diocese with professional and other organisations on matters connected with the inspection and repair of places of worship, including the appointment of architects and surveyors.

PART III

RECOMMENDED MODEL CODE OF BUSINESS AND PROCEDURE FOR A DIOCESAN ADVISORY COMMITTEE

Prefatory Note

This model code is adapted from that set out in Appendix 5 to the Faculty Jurisdiction Commission Report *The Continuing Care of Churches and Cathedrals*. It deals primarily with those cases where a formal application for advice has been made to the DAC under r.3 of the Faculty Jurisdiction Rules before a petition for a faculty is lodged. It should, however, be read within the context of the general responsibility of every DAC to be an educator, as well as an adviser on *ad hoc* problems, a duty to which Schedule 2 to the 1991 Measure attaches considerable weight. If parishes can be encouraged to turn to the DAC for help and advice on an informal basis in the very earliest stages of an important or complex project, their case is much more likely to run smoothly when the formal application has been lodged, and any signs of future conflict can very often be resolved in personal dialogue.

Applications for advice, business and procedure

.1   *Submission of application:* Parishes should be encouraged to minute their own discussions of any proposed faculty application and to notify their considered views, with their voting figures, to the DAC with the application.

2   *Site visits* are also of the first importance. A programme of visits prior to the discussion of cases by the full DAC can be helpful as a means of handling this systematically. In the long term visits can actually prevent delays by ensuring that all relevant information is obtained *before* an application comes to the DAC for consideration, so that it can be dealt with at a single meeting. Where a site visit has taken place, the DAC should receive an oral, or preferably, a written report – see para. 12 – on the visit at the meeting at which the relevant application is to be considered. The parish and all others concerned should be told that, whatever comments may have been made during the visit, they do not bind the DAC, and that the DAC as a whole (or a committee of the DAC where applicable – see para. 4) will need to consider the matter before giving advice.

3   *Meetings* should be held as frequently as is necessary to allow cases to be handled without undue delay, and should be convened by the secretary in consultation with the chairman (or the standing committee, if any). The DAC should also have a procedure

for dealing with *urgent cases* (although this must always involve a written notification of the decision on Form 1 in Appendix B to the Faculty Jurisdiction Rules). The ordering of the DAC's business will depend to a large extent upon the system of sub-committees adopted, or upon the existence of a standing committee.

4 *Sub-committees:* Some dioceses may find it helpful to have a standing committee or sub-committee able to give preliminary consideration to some applications. For example, in a very large diocese, sub-committees constituted on an area or archdeaconry basis may be needed to co-ordinate an adequate programme of visits. If the total volume of work reaching the DAC is considerable, or if swift action is to be taken, it may be necessary for a sub-committee to be entrusted with powers almost as extensive as those of the full committee. Bearing in mind the careful stipulations about the composition of the full committee laid down in the 1991 Measure, every effort should be made to ensure that sub-committees are constituted, so far as possible, with due regard to the same principles. Their members should of course be drawn from members of the full committee.

5 *Time taken for consideration:* After the DAC has received a formal application for advice, the responsibility for its future progress rests with the committee. The aim should be to deal with straightforward cases within two months. There will be cases where more time is required, in particular where further expert advice is needed from the Council for the Care of Churches or some other person or body, but no case should be allowed to 'drop out of sight'.

6 *Notice:* The preparation of the DAC agenda will require a closing date for receipt of applications for each meeting, and this could be publicised by an information leaflet circulated to parishes annually.

7 *The agenda:* The content of the agenda should be determined by the secretary in consultation with the standing committee or the chairman, as appropriate, and should be posted or delivered to every member and consultant, together with the necessary briefing material (see also para. 10) at least ten days before the meeting. Save for urgent or other specially important business added by direction of the chairman, no business should be considered at a meeting other than that specified in the agenda or arising from business so specified. Certain items of business may need to be timed on the agenda.

8 *Notifying amenity societies and Council for the Care of Churches:* Copies of the agenda and minutes should automatically be circulated to the National Amenity Societies, to the Council for the Care of Churches and to such local societies as the DAC itself may decide, not less than ten days before the date of each DAC meeting. A copy of the agenda of each DAC meeting should be available for inspection at the same place as the register of faculty petitions maintained under s.15(3) of the 1991 Measure. (These provisions should be in addition to the normal citation provisions.) A society wishing to know more about a particular case should write to the secretary prior to the meeting,

sending a copy of the letter to the diocesan registrar so that the registrar is aware of the society's interest.

9   *Attendance:* It is important that so far as possible there should be a fully adequate attendance of members, including the archdeacons, at each meeting of the DAC, to ensure a balanced decision. It may be desirable on occasion, particularly in important or complex cases, for ministers, parochial representatives or their professional advisers who are not on the DAC to be invited to attend to explain their proposals. Such visitors should, however, always withdraw before a decision is taken, and this requirement should apply equally to any member of the DAC, e.g. a practising architect, who has a direct interest in a scheme under consideration. The onus should be on each member to declare any special interest, and the minutes should record that the member concerned has done so and did not take part in the decision.

10   *Briefing material:* Briefing of members should be sufficiently early to allow them time to study the cases privately, before meetings. Wherever possible, the secretary or another member of the committee should circulate a written report summarising the background and issues relating to the case. Ideally the background material should also be made available, and should include all material submitted with the application, including any representations from the applicants, and all necessary plans, drawings and photographs, as well as notes on the previous case history of the buildings involved, including any relevant extracts from quinquennial inspection reports and, where available, copies of any grant applications. In order to save expense it may be necessary for some material to be laid out for inspection a few hours before the meeting, rather than circulated to all members. Where necessary and possible, representatives of the DAC should have visited churches etc. prior to the meetings at which they will be discussed.

11   *Archives:* Full and systematic records are an invaluable briefing aid and therefore it is desirable that every DAC should build up a comprehensive archive of all the churches and places of worship in the diocese. For every building there should be a survey and reference file, as well as a correspondence file; the former should contain copies of the list description (in the case of a listed building), quinquennial inspection reports, specifications and drawings which have come before the committee (if submitted in duplicate), details of faculty petitions sent to the secretary under r.10 of the Faculty Jurisdiction Rules and the outcome of petitions, photographs, and perhaps occasional engravings or other visual evidence of the buildings. The archive should also include the standard printed works on church architecture and ecclesiology and include especially those works which relate to churches in the diocese (or county) concerned. In some instances, reference may helpfully be made to local authority records, to cathedral libraries, to the Council for the Care of Churches' archive and to the National Monuments Records. Duplicates may on occasion be obtained from one of these sources at reasonable cost.

12 *Presentation of cases:* The officer or member most familiar with the case should introduce it orally and draw attention to the most significant features of the building and the most salient points of the case. If the proposal is for alterations, additions, or the introduction of new furnishings or works of art, then drawings, models or maquettes, and other visual evidence (as appropriate) will be essential. Photographs should also be made available of the church itself so that committee members can judge the context in which the changes are being proposed. When a delegation has visited, or in difficult cases where other preliminary consultation has taken place, it is generally desirable that a brief *written* report should be presented to the committee, and that a note by any appropriate specialist adviser should be appended to it.

13 *Discussion and decision making:* The quorum required by the DAC's constitution must be present. Although a substantial amount of preparatory work may have been carried out in the sub-committees, the final decision must be taken by the full DAC or a sub-committee to which power to deal 'with the matter has been formally delegated. It is particularly helpful if the DAC can make a *corporate judgement*, based on a consensus of opinion, on as many cases as possible. Nevertheless, subject to the provisions of the constitution, a decision may be carried by a simple majority of the committee, the chairman having the same voting rights as other members and having no second or casting vote. As mentioned in para. 9, members with a direct interest in a particular case should *not* be present when a final decision is made on it, nor should they be able to vote on it. If, however, a particular expert is absent from a discussion involving the relevant expertise. the decision may be made subject to that expert advice. Where the DAC decides to recommend approval or raise no objection, that may be subject to provisos (for example as to suggested conditions).

14 *Reporting decisions:* The DAC's minutes and minutes of sub-committees should be full and explanatory: this is especially important where the committee has been narrowly divided; where specialised expert opinion differs; or where the committee has decided not to recommend the application. If, in that event, the applicant nevertheless petitions for a faculty, the committee should be able to assure the chancellor that the applicant's views have been fully considered. Decisions should be notified to applicants in Form 1 of Appendix B to the Faculty Jurisdiction Rules, and where the proposals are not recommended the principal reasons should be fully and carefully explained. All sub-committee minutes should be circulated to the full committee.

15 *Disputed cases:* The DAC will ordinarily have a responsibility to ensure that any relevant expert opinion is available to the chancellor and that a member of the committee will be available to give oral evidence in the consistory court, if required.

Duties of the secretary

16 The duties of the secretary shall (*inter alia*) be as follows:

to decide the division of cases between the full committee and any sub-committee(s) in consultation with the chairman;

to prepare and circulate agendas;

to prepare cases for presentation to the DAC;

to keep full *explanatory* minutes;

to supervise the keeping of records (including the DAC's archives);

to arrange site visits;

to prepare budget applications in consultation with the chairman;

to maintain contact and foster good relations with (a) the *parishes* (the DAC secretary should be the principal contact for the parishes); and (b) the Council for the Care of Churches and other national and local bodies of standing having an interest in churches, e.g. amenity societies, local planning authorities, wildlife bodies;

–   to attend the annual DAC conference;

–   to maintain the register of petitions required by the 1991 Measure.

Liaison

17   *At diocesan level:* Decisions taken in one part of the diocese must not hamper or conflict with those taken in other parts. The DAC should take special care to maintain liaison with the Diocesan Pastoral Committee, the Diocesan Redundant Churches Uses Committee and Furnishings Officer, and the Diocesan Liturgical Committee or Worship Committee. In addition to liaison with local amenity societies and wildlife bodies, close liaison should also be maintained with the appropriate local government authorities.

18   *At national level:* In addition to liaison with National Amenity Societies and English Heritage the DAC should maintain close contact with the Council for the Care of Churches. It should also keep abreast of any advances in knowledge or other changes which may be relevant to their work.

19   *The bishop and chancellor* should be invited to meet the DAC from time to time, e.g. annually, to discuss matters of policy and public relations.

20   *The registrar* should send to the DAC and the archdeacon monthly consolidated lists of:

(a)   faculties granted and refused; and

(b)   completed works.

The archdeacon may in turn notify the rural dean, for monitoring purposes.

21 *The archdeacons* are uniquely placed between the parishes, the legal officers, the Diocesan Board of Finance, the Diocesan Pastoral Committee and the DAC, and this position should be used to the full.

22 *Introduction to new incumbents:* The DAC should introduce itself and its range of concerns to new incumbents, preferably by letter. Similar material should also be made available to new DAC members. Occasional 'teach-ins' at deanery level could also be helpful for this purpose.

An annual leaflet should be sent to all incumbents and PCCs containing dates of meetings in the coming year, closing dates for applications, general procedural advice and topical information. A leaflet on procedure should also be sent to parishes and additional copies kept available to be handed out as necessary.

An annual tour for the DAC, e.g. covering a different deanery or archdeaconry each year, is a further possibility.

The DAC should also participate in *training days for churchwardens* and take active steps to *disseminate information* about its work throughout the diocese.

Annual Reports
23 Under the provisions of s. 2(7) of the 1991 Measure, the DAC must submit an annual report to the diocesan synod. It is better if, in addition to summarising the year's work, the annual report is used to explain the objects of the DAC, and the opportunity is taken to refer to diocesan policy in relation to any of the DAC's functions.

Inspecting architects and surveyors
24 The DAC has a statutory duty to approve *architects and surveyors* to carry out quinquennial inspections under the Inspection of Churches Measure 1955 and may bear in mind as a general principle in making its selections the character of individual churches. The committee should keep the list of names under regular review (e.g. not less than annually), and should take the initiative in organising annual or biennial one-day conferences etc. for approved architects and surveyors to allow the free exchange of information and ideas and perhaps to provide an element of specialist training.

Insurance
25 Every DAC should make adequate provision for *indemnifying or insuring its members*. Advice should be sought on this from the Council for the Care of Churches.

Other matters
26 The Code for each diocese should, for example, cover the DAC's *financial business* (the preparation of its budget and accounts, and their presentation to the diocese).

APPENDIX B
FACULTY PROCEDURE – FLOWCHART

(These flow charts, subject to a few minor modifications, were produced by Mrs. Mary
Saunders, the Secretary of the Oxford DAC, and her husband Dr. David Saunders; their
help is gratefully acknowledged).

References:
- s. = section in 1991 Measure
- r. = rule in Faculty Jurisdiction ruler 1992
- Form = Form in Appendix B to Faculty Jurisdiction Ruler 1992
- § = paragraph

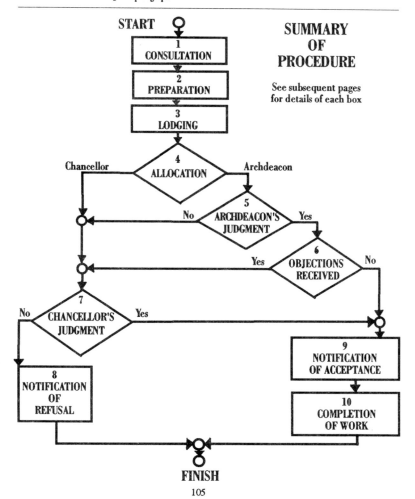

START

SUMMARY OF PROCEDURE

See subsequent pages
for details of each box

1 CONSULTATION

2 PREPARATION

3 LODGING

4 ALLOCATION — Chancellor / Archdeacon

5 ARCHDEACON'S JUDGMENT — No / Yes

6 OBJECTIONS RECEIVED — Yes / No

7 CHANCELLOR'S JUDGMENT — No / Yes

8 NOTIFICATION OF REFUSAL

9 NOTIFICATION OF ACCEPTANCE

10 COMPLETION OF WORK

FINISH

1. CONSULTATION

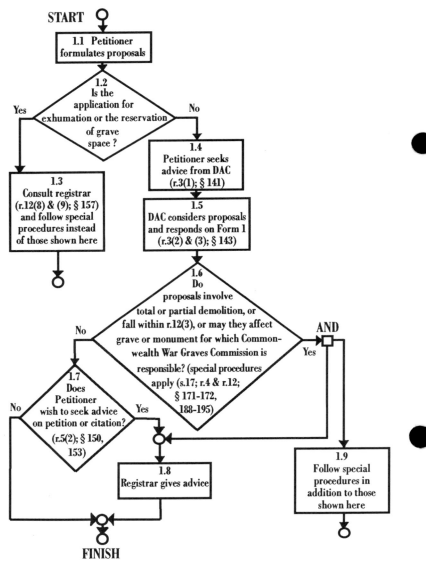

START

1.1 Petitioner formulates proposals

1.2 Is the application for exhumation or the reservation of grave space ?

Yes → **1.3** Consult registrar (r.12(8) & (9); § 157) and follow special procedures instead of those shown here

No → **1.4** Petitioner seeks advice from DAC (r.3(1); § 141)

1.5 DAC considers proposals and responds on Form 1 (r.3(2) & (3); § 143)

1.6 Do proposals involve total or partial demolition, or fall within r.12(3), or may they affect grave or monument for which Commonwealth War Graves Commission is responsible? (special procedures apply (s.17; r.4 & r.12; § 171-172, 188-195)

No → **1.7** Does Petitioner wish to seek advice on petition or citation? (r.5(2); § 150, 153)

Yes / AND

1.8 Registrar gives advice

1.9 Follow special procedures in addition to those shown here

FINISH

2. PREPARATION

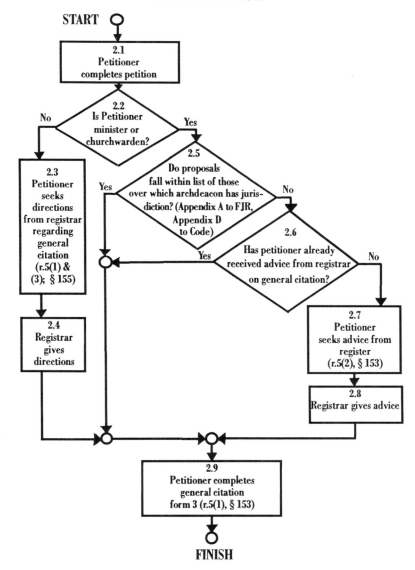

START

2.1
Petitioner
completes petition

2.2
Is Petitioner
minister or
churchwarden?

No — **2.3**
Petitioner
seeks
directions
from registrar
regarding
general
citation
(r.5(1) &
(3); § 155)

Yes — **2.5**
Do proposals
fall within list of those
over which archdeacon has jurisdiction? (Appendix A to FJR,
Appendix D
to Code)

Yes / No

2.6
Has petitioner already
received advice from registrar
on general citation?

Yes / No

2.4
Registrar
gives
directions

2.7
Petitioner
seeks advice from
register
(r.5(2), § 153)

2.8
Registrar gives advice

2.9
Petitioner completes
general citation
form 3 (r.5(1), § 153)

FINISH

3. LODGING

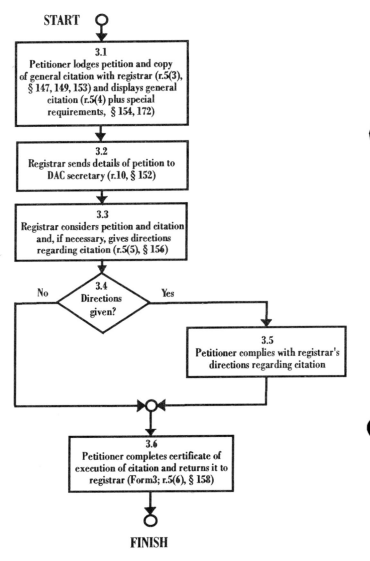

START

3.1
Petitioner lodges petition and copy of general citation with registrar (r.5(3), § 147, 149, 153) and displays general citation (r.5(4) plus special requirements, § 154, 172)

3.2
Registrar sends details of petition to DAC secretary (r.10, § 152)

3.3
Registrar considers petition and citation and, if necessary, gives directions regarding citation (r.5(5), § 156)

3.4
Directions given?

No   Yes

3.5
Petitioner complies with registrar's directions regarding citation

3.6
Petitioner completes certificate of execution of citation and returns it to registrar (Form3; r.5(6), § 158)

FINISH

4. ALLOCATION

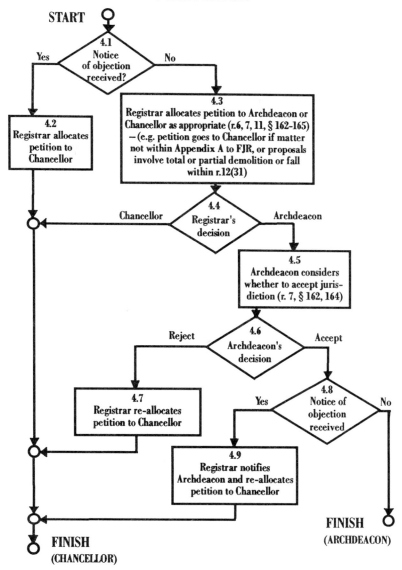

START

4.1 Notice of objection received?

Yes → No

4.2 Registrar allocates petition to Chancellor

4.3 Registrar allocates petition to Archdeacon or Chancellor as appropriate (r.6, 7, 11, § 162-165) – (e.g. petition goes to Chancellor if matter not within Appendix A to FJR, or proposals involve total or partial demolition or fall within r.12(31)

4.4 Registrar's decision

Chancellor / Archdeacon

4.5 Archdeacon considers whether to accept juris-diction (r. 7, § 162, 164)

4.6 Archdeacon's decision

Reject / Accept

4.7 Registrar re-allocates petition to Chancellor

4.8 Notice of objection received

Yes / No

4.9 Registrar notifies Archdeacon and re-allocates petition to Chancellor

FINISH (ARCHDEACON)

FINISH (CHANCELLOR)

5. ARCHDEACON'S JUDGMENT

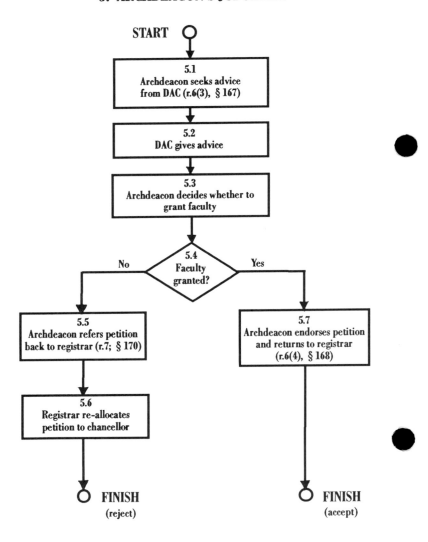

START

5.1
Archdeacon seeks advice
from DAC (r.6(3), § 167)

5.2
DAC gives advice

5.3
Archdeacon decides whether to
grant faculty

5.4
Faculty
granted?

No — Yes

5.5
Archdeacon refers petition
back to registrar (r.7; § 170)

5.7
Archdeacon endorses petition
and returns to registrar
(r.6(4), § 168)

5.6
Registrar re-allocates
petition to chancellor

FINISH
(reject)

FINISH
(accept)

6. OBJECTIONS RECEIVED

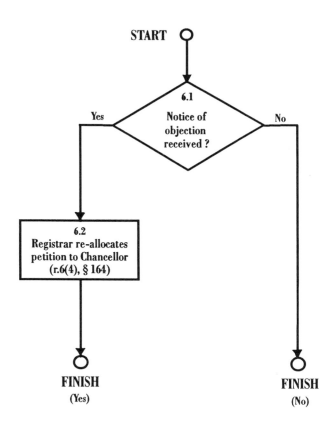

START ○

6.1
Notice of
objection
received ?

Yes

No

6.2
Registrar re-allocates
petition to Chancellor
(r.6(4), § 164)

FINISH
(Yes)

FINISH
(No)

7. CHANCELLOR'S JUDGMENT

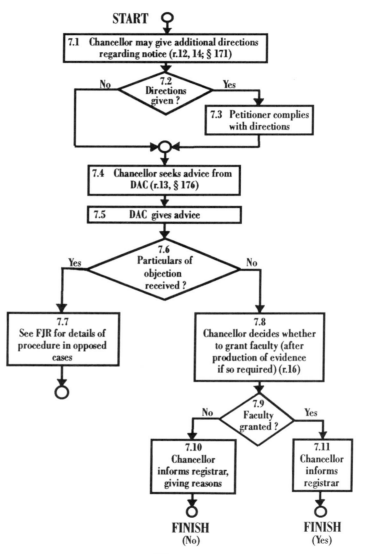

START

7.1 Chancellor may give additional directions regarding notice (r.12, 14; § 171)

7.2 Directions given ?

No

Yes

7.3 Petitioner complies with directions

7.4 Chancellor seeks advice from DAC (r.13, § 176)

7.5 DAC gives advice

7.6 Particulars of objection received ?

Yes

No

7.7 See FJR for details of procedure in opposed cases

7.8 Chancellor decides whether to grant faculty (after production of evidence if so required) (r.16)

7.9 Faculty granted ?

No

Yes

7.10 Chancellor informs registrar, giving reasons

7.11 Chancellor informs registrar

FINISH (No)

FINISH (Yes)

8. NOTIFICATION OF REFUSAL

START ⚲

8.1 Registrar gives notice of decision and reasons to petitioner, DAC secretary, those who have been specially cited and have commented, and English Heritage and CCC if they have applied to give evidence (also all objectors in opposed cases) (§ 182)

FINISH

9. NOTIFICATION OF ACCEPTANCE

START ⚲

9.1 Registrar issues faculty (Form 5) and blank certificate of completion (Form 6) to petitioner (r.6(4), § 168, 182) and notifies DAC secretary, those who have been specially cited and have commented, and English Hertitage and CCC if they have applied to give evidence (also all objectors in opposed cases) (§ 182)

FINISH

10. COMPLETION OF WORK

START ⚲

10.1 Petitioner carries out works, etc. authorised by faculty, in accordance with any conditions

10.2 Petitioner fills in certificate of completion and returns it to registrar

10.3 Registrar notifies DAC secretary (§ 168, 182)

 FINISH

APPENDIX C

FACULTY PETITION

(Faculty Jurisdiction Rules, Appendix B Form No. 2)

To the Consistory Court of the Diocese of ....

Parish of ....

Church of ....

We

State in respect of each petitioner in capital letters (a) full name (b) residential address and (c) office held (e.g. churchwarden)

Petition as follows:

1.   The Petitioners seek a faculty authorising the works or purposes described in the Schedule hereto.

2.   The particulars of the works or purposes are accurately shown in the designs, plans, specification or other documents accompanying this petition.

3.   *(i) An *estimate/quotation has been obtained for the works or purposes in the sum of £   from the contractor or supplier named in the answer to Question 10 below, *or*

      *(ii) The architect or surveyor who has been engaged in respect of the works or purposes has indicated the cost as being of the order of £   , *or*

      *(iii) No *estimate/quotation/indication of cost has been obtained for the works or purposes.

4.   *(i) The Parochial Church Council will contribute to the cost of the works or purposes the sum of approximately £   which it has immediately available from the following sources, *or*

      *(ii) The Parochial Church Council proposes to raise any balance in the following ways, *or*

      *(iii) The works or purposes will be paid for privately or by way of gifts which have already been made or promised.

* *Delete that which does not apply*

114

5.	The Parochial Church Council at its meeting on passed [*unanimously] [*without dissent] [*by a majority of to among those present and voting] a resolution relating to the works or purposes. A copy of such resolution signed by the [*Chairman] [*Secretary] is attached to this Petition. There are members of the Council.

6.	The Diocesan Advisory Committee [*has] [*has not] been consulted in relation to the works or purposes. A certificate from the Committee [*accompanies][*does not accompany] this petition.

Delete that which does not apply

SCHEDULE OF WORKS OR PURPOSES

(Please set out clearly in numbered paragraphs what you want leave to do.)

NOTES FOR COMPLETING SCHEDULE

*1.	You must set out a clear summary of the works or purposes and the petition should be accompanied by all relevant plans, specifications and other documents identifying the works or purposes to be undertaken.*

*2.	The reference number and date on the architect's or surveyor's drawing[s] and specification[s] should be included adjacent to the description of the works or purposes to which they refer. All documents lodged with the Petition will be retained in the registry after the issue of the faculty.*

*3.	The subject and position of any window, tablet or other memorial and the wording and style of any inscription should be included.*

*4.	Where the advice of the Diocesan Advisory Committee has been obtained the works or purposes must be the same as those described in the certificate from the Committee.*

*5.	Any faculty granted on this petition can only authorise works or purposes which are clearly included in the schedule.*

QUESTIONS

Such of these questions as apply to the case are to be answered by the Petitioners. Any question that is not applicable should be marked "N/A". If the answer to any question cannot conveniently be fitted in the space provided a separate piece of paper duly identified should be used.

QUESTION	ANSWER
1. What is the approximate date of the building?	
2. (a) Is the building listed as a building of historic or architectural interest under the Planning (Listed Buildings and Conservation Areas) Act 1990?	YES/NO
(b) If *yes*, state of what grade.	
3. (a) Has any previous faculty or archdeacon's certificate, relevant to the present proposals, been sought or granted?	YES/NO
(b) If yes, give date and other details.	
4. (a) Is grant aid being sought from English Heritage?	YES/NO
(b) If yes, attach copies of correspondence including copies of any application and any offer of assistance or grant.	
5. (a) Has the building previously been the subject of a grant from English Heritage, or one of its predecessors?	YES/NO
(b) If yes, have the present proposals been reported to English Heritage?	YES/NO
(c) If so, state with what result. If appropriate, please send copies of any relevant correspondence showing that English Heritage agrees with the specification for the works proposed.	
6. (a) If any external works to the building are proposed, has outline or detailed planning permission been sought?	YES/NO

(b) If yes, with what result? Please supply a copy of any planning permission or notice of refusal.

7. (a) Is any part of the building to be demolished?   YES/NO

   (b) If yes, which ground or grounds under section 17 of the Care of Churches and Ecclesiastical Jurisdiction Measure 1991 are relied upon?

8. If work to a churchyard, or other land occupied with the church, is involved in the works or purposes:

   (i) is the land in question consecrated or unconsecrated?

   (ii) has any part of the land on which the works will take place ever been used for burials?   YES/NO

   (iii) is any part of the churchyard or other land occupied with the church still being used for burials?   YES/NO

   (iv) if the churchyard is no longer in use, has it been closed by Order in Council?   YES/NO

9. (a) Who is the architect or surveyor appointed for the church in question under the Inspection of Churches Measure 1955?

   (b) Has this architect or surveyor been:
     (i) instructed, or   YES/NO
     (ii) consulted in relation to the proposed works?   YES/NO

   (c) If another architect or surveyor is to be employed:
     (i) state his name and address
     (ii) why is he being instructed in relation to the proposed works?

10. What are the names and addresses of the contractor, builder, electrical engineer, organ builder, artist or other person instructed to carry out the proposed works?

11. If the proposed works would affect the organ, the electrical installation or will affect the security of the building against fire, vandalism, theft or other risks, has the consent of the insurers of the church been sought?   YES/NO

A copy of the insurers' approval or other reply must be submitted.

12. (i) Do bats use any part of the church?   YES/NO

(ii) If yes, do you or your architect think that the works or purposes might harm or disturb bats or their roosts?   YES/NO

(iii) If the answer to (ii) is yes, have you obtained advice or a licence from English Nature?   YES/NO

(Please supply copy of licence or advice.)

13. (a) How soon will work start after a faculty is granted?

(b) After work has been started, how long will it take for the work to be completed?

14. If works inside a church are proposed
(a) (i) will any graves, monuments, or inscriptions be affected?   YES/NO

(ii) if yes, how?

(iii) have the owners consented and on what terms?

(iv) if the owners have not been found, what efforts have been made to find them?

(b) (i) if a commemorative plaque or other memorial is proposed to be introduced into the church, what special contribution has been made by the person to be commemorated to the life of the Church, country or mankind?

     (ii)   are there any relevant
            circumstances as to that person's
            local connections or services?

(c) (i)   will divine service be interrupted?   YES/NO

    (ii) if yes, what alternative
          arrangements are proposed?

(d) (i)   are any private rights in seats
          likely to be affected?   YES/NO

    (ii) if yes, have the owners consented
          and on what terms?

15. (a) Is the disposal of any item of church
        property contemplated?   YES/NO

   (b) Has a professional valuation been
        obtained?   YES/NO

   (c) If yes, supply a copy.

   (d) If not, what is the Petitioners' estimate
        of the value of the item?

   (e) How do the Petitioners propose to
        dispose of it?

   (f) What do the Petitioners wish to be
        authorised to do with any proceeds of sale?

16. (a) Is work to a churchyard proposed?   YES/NO

   (b) If yes, will any graves, reserved grave
        spaces, monuments or inscriptions be
        interfered with?   YES/NO

(c) (i)   How will they be dealt with?

    (ii) To what extent do the owners
          consent and on what terms?

    (iii) If the owners have not been
           found what efforts have been made
           to find them?

Note: In dealing with this question the consent
        of known near relatives should be sought
        as if they were owners.

(d) (i)   Will there be interference with a grave
          containing a burial made between 1914
          and 1947? If so what is the name of the
          deceased and date of burial?

    (ii)   Will there be interference with a
memorial commemorating a death
between 1914 and 1947? If so what is
the name of the person commemorated
and date of death?

    (iii) Does the grave in (i) or (ii) appear to
be a War Grave?   YES/NO

    (iv) Does the Commonwealth War
Graves Commission consent?   YES/NO

         (Please attach any letter of consent.)

 (e) Is any such monument listed as being of
historic or architectural interest under
the Planning (Listed Buildings and
Conservation Areas) Act 1990?   YES/NO

17. (a) If work to a chancel is proposed, is
there a Lay Rector?   YES/NO

 (b) If so, state his or her name and address.

 (c) Has the Lay Rector been informed of
the work?   YES/NO

 (d) Is he or she intending to contribute to the
cost?   YES/NO

18 (a) Is there any further information which
the Petitioners would like the Court to
take into account?   YES/NO

 (b) If yes, please set out in an accompanying
statement or letter.

**The statements in this Petition and the answers to the questions above are true to
the best of the knowledge and belief of each one of us.**

Date: .... 19 ....

....

....

(Signatures of Petitioners)

**Please ensure that you have answered all relevant questions; otherwise the petition
may have to be returned to you for completion thus causing delay.**

APPENDIX D

FACULTY MATTERS WITHIN THE ARCHDEACON'S JURISDICTION
(APPENDIX A TO THE FACULTY JURISDICTION RULES)

The Archdeacon has jurisdiction in faculty matters in respect of any of the matters set out below which affect any parish church, licensed building, consecrated chapel, curtilage of such building or churchyard (whether consecrated or not), which is within the jurisdiction of the consistory court.

1. WORK TO THE FABRIC

    (i)   Minor structural alterations not involving demolition or partial demolition, except where in the opinion of the advisory committee they will result in a material alteration either externally or internally to the appearance of the church or affect its setting and provided that where state aid has previously been accepted or is being sought a letter from English Heritage stating that that body agrees with the specification for any works proposed to be carried out is obtained prior to the grant of a faculty;

    (ii)   repairs (using matching materials) and treatment of timber against beetle or fungal activity;

    (iii)   external or internal decoration or redecoration except where in the opinion of the advisory committee it will result in a material alteration either externally or internally to the appearance of the church.

2. WORK AFFECTING FIXTURES

    (a) Repairs

        (i)   repairs and alterations to an existing heating system;

        (ii)   repairs to and redecoration of fixtures (with matching materials);

        (iii)   repairs to broken or cracked quarries in clear glazed windows;

        (iv)   repairs, rewiring and minor alterations to an existing electrical system;

        (v)   repairs to lightning conductors;

        (vi)   repairs to organs or harmoniums using matching materials;

        (vii)   repairs using matching materials to bells and bell frames and replacement of parts not requiring the removal of the bells from their frames;

        (viii) repairs using matching materials to and redecoration of clocks and clock faces;

        (ix)   treatment of fixtures against beetle or fungal activity.

121

(b) New Work

(i)   installation of a new heating system including laying of electrical cables, gas pipes or water mains through the churchyard (except where in the opinion of the advisory committee the installation will affect the archaeological interest of or will result in a material alteration to the appearance of the church);

(ii)   installation of a sound reinforcement system or loop system or alteration to an existing system;

(iii)   installation of a new electrical system or lighting including laying of electrical cables through the churchyard (except where in the opinion of the advisory committee the installation will affect the archaeological interest or result in a material alteration to the appearance of the church);

(iv)   installation of a wall offertory box (except where in the opinion of the advisory committee the installation will affect the archaeological interest of or will result in a material alteration to the appearance of the church);

(v)   installation of a wall safe in a vestry (except where in the opinion of the advisory committee it will affect the archaeological importance of the church);

(vi)   installation of a lightning conductor.

3.   WORK AFFECTING MOVABLES

(i)   Introduction of any article which may lawfully be used in the performance of divine service or the rites of the Church (other than an aumbry);

(ii)   repairs to movables (using matching materials) not including Royal Coats of Arms, unfixed hatchments, heraldic achievements, paintings, historic textiles, historic silver and base metal work;

(iii)   installation of minor items of furniture or minor fixtures in the church;

(iv)   provision of carpets and curtains;

(v)   introduction of altar frontals and falls;

(vi)   a scheme for replacement of all or a substantial number of hassocks;

(vii)   laying up of banners;

(vii)   introduction of a Book of Remembrance and a stand for it;

(ix)   security marking of movables.

122

4. WORK AFFECTING CHURCHYARDS

(i) Re-surfacing of paths in the same material resulting in the same appearance;

(ii) repairs to walls, fences, gates and lych gates where matching materials are to be used;

(iii) introduction of a garden seat (including any memorial inscription);

(iv) provision or replacement or repainting in a new colour scheme of a noticeboard;

(v) placing of floodlights and the laying of associated cables in the churchyard to illuminate the church.

APPENDIX E

FACULTY JURISDICTION COMMISSION RECOMMENDATIONS ON CONTENTS OF CHURCHES

(The paragraphs that follow are taken from the Summary of Recommendations in the Faculty Jurisdiction Commission report *The Continuing Care of Churches and Cathedrals*.)

Additional Contents

179. DACs should be in a position to supply parishes who wish to commission new work with information about the available registers of artists, workshops, art colleges and art associations.

180. A DAC should view an artist's working drawings with imagination and never reject his work with no reason given.

181. DACs should be available to help parishes to organise projects which involve the borrowing of works of art through the Arts Council, and the use of exhibition space inside a church for this and similar purposes.

182. Parishioners should be (i) encouraged to contribute money to large and worthwhile projects rather than give small individual items, possibly not required, and (ii) advised that where such gifts are contributed by way of memorial the name of the person commemorated can helpfully be recorded in a parish Memorial Book.

Disposals

186. Parishes should be advised (i) to advertise a sale in the specialist Press; (ii) to take the advice of the DAC on the terms of both advertisement and sale.

188. A code of practice for chancellors should contain certain practical advice on the merits of loans rather than sales, on the preservation of sets or collections and on the financing of repairs prior to sale.

Contents of Redundant Churches

189. Diocesan Boards of Finance should not ignore the continued application of the faculty jurisdiction during the waiting period or, in doing so, delegate authority for disposals/removals entirely to the Diocesan Furnishings Officer.

190. Transfers for safekeeping (which are allowed without faculty under section 49(2)(b) of the Pastoral Measure 1983) should not be undertaken where the items cannot be moved without some destruction.

191. A chancellor before granting a faculty for alienation should require all the ordinary conditions relative to alienation from a church in use to be satisfied and there should be a strong presumption against sale until the future of the buildings is resolved.

192. Every DAC should recognise that it has a legal responsibility to advise the Diocesan Board of Finance on sales during the waiting period, and it should be generally appreciated that the Council for the Care of Churches has the same standing in regard to disposals or removals during this period as at other times.

195. Dioceses should try (i) to appoint new Diocesan Furnishings Officers with relevant qualifications and experience and a sympathy for the subject; (ii) to encourage Diocesan Furnishings Officers who lack training to attend an approved course.

APPENDIX F

FACULTY AND COURT FEES (AS FROM 1ST MARCH 1993)

(TABLE I OF THE SCHEDULE TO THE ECCLESIASTICAL JUDGES AND LEGAL OFFICERS (FEES) ORDER 1992)

		Dean of the Arches, Vicar General or Chancellor £	Registrar or other Officers by usage performing the duty £
	Note: The figures in this Appendix do not include VAT, which is payable in addition where applicable.		
1.	Archdeacon's Faculty. Fee payable on lodging petition (rule 3).	—	35
2.	Chancellor's Faculty. Fees payable on lodging petition (rule 3).	25	55
3.	Additional fees where the Chancellor has ordered under rule 25 that the proceedings are to be determined upon consideration of written representations, such fees, and by whom they are to be paid, to be fixed by the Chancellor within the limits shown.	88 – 139	56 – 83
4.	On the registrar referring a petition in respect of which a fee has become payable under paragraph 1 of this Table to the Chancellor under rule 6(5), 7 or 9, the petitioner, if he wishes to proceed, shall pay a further fee of	25	20
5.	Additional fees on the Judge or registrar giving other directions (otherwise than at a hearing in respect of which fees are payable under paragraph 6 of this Table), such fees, and by whom they are to be paid, to be fixed by the Judge within the limits shown –		
	(a) on a pre-trial review of the case as a whole under rule 18 –	53 –159	35 –106
	(i) directions given by Judge		
	(ii) directions given by registrar	—	53 –159

126

	Dean of the Arches, Vicar General or Chancellor	Registrar or other Officers by usage performing the duty
	£	£
(b) on the giving of other directions –	21-64	
(i) directions given by Judge		14 - 42
(ii) directions given by registrar		21 - 64

6. Additional fees where the issue, whether opposed or unopposed, whether interlocutory or final, is to be heard in Court or in Chambers before the Chancellor's Court, the Court of Arches or Chancery Court or York, or the Court of Ecclesiastical Causes Reserved –

(a) if the case lasts half a day or less	166	125
(b) if the case lasts a whole day or more than half	278	209

(fees on same scale for subsequent days)

7. Additional fee on the Judge preparing a written judgement or drafting the form of order or both, such fee to be at the hourly rate shown and in respect of the number of hours certified by the Judge as spent in such work, and by whom the fee is to be paid to be determined by the Court.

27	–

8. Preparatory and ancillary work and correspondence (if any) in relation to petition for faculty – not to exceed without the sanction of the Judge.

–	25

9. (a) No fees are payable under paragraphs 5 and 6 to the members of the Court of Ecclesiastical Causes Reserved.

(b) All other fees of the Registry in opposed cases are to be paid on the same scale as allowed for Court fees, from time to time, in the Supreme Court of Judicature.

(c) 'Judge' means the Chancellor or Presiding Judge of the Appellate Court.

(d) References to Rules are to the Faculty Jursidiction Rules 1992.

127

APPENDIX G

USEFUL NAMES AND ADDRESSES

Church Bodies

Council for the Care of Churches, 83 London Wall, London EC2M 5NA
(tel. 071 638 0971; fax 071 638 0184)

Church Commissioners, 1 Millbank, London SW1P 3JZ
(tel. 071 222 7010; fax 071 222 5490)

Liturgical Commission, Church House, Great Smith Street, London SW1P 3NZ
(tel. 071 222 9011; fax 071 233 2660)

The names, addresses and telephone numbers of the diocesan registrar and DAC
secretary of each diocese will be found in the Diocesan Year Book or Handbook and in
the *Church of England Year Book* (published by Church House Publishing)

National Bodies General

English Heritage, Fortress House, 23 Savile Row, London W1X 1AB
(tel. 071 973 3000; fax 071 973 3001)

Commonwealth War Graves Commission, 2 Marlow Road, Maidenhead, Berkshire
SL6 7DX (tel. 0628 34221; fax 0628 771208)

Royal Commission on the Historical Monuments of England, Fortress House, 23 Savile
Row, London W1X 1AB (tel. 071 973 3500; fax 071 494 3998)

National Association of Decorative and Fine Art Societies (NADFAS), 8a Lower
Grosvenor Place, London SW1W 0EN (tel. 071 233 5433; fax 071 233 8250)

Royal Institute of British Architects, 66 Portland Place, London W1N 4AD
(tel. 071 580 5533; fax 071 255 1541)

Royal Institution of Chartered Surveyors, 12 Great George Street, London SW1P 3AD
(tel. 071 222 7000; fax 071 222 9430)

Ecclesiastical Architects and Surveyors Association, c/o David Clark, Scan House, 29
Radnor Cliff, Folkestone, Kent CT20 2JJ (tel. 0227 459401; fax 0227 450964)

Association for Studies in the Conservation of Historic Buildings, c/o Mrs Margaret
Davies, 20A Hartington Road, Chiswick, London W4 3UA (tel. 081 994 2803)

Amenity Societies

Joint Committee of the National Amenity Societies, St Ann's Vestry Hall, 2 Church Entry, London EC4V 5HB (tel. 071 236 3934; fax 071 329 3677)

The Ancient Monuments Society, St Ann's Vestry Hall, 2 Church Entry, London EC4V 5HB (tel. 071 236 3934; fax 071 329 3677)

The Council for British Archaeology: London office: 112 Kennington Road, London SE11 6RE (tel. 071 582 0494; fax 071 587 5152);

York office (deals with case work): Bowes Morrell House, 111 Walmgate, York YO1 2UA (tel. 0904 671417; fax. 0904 671384)

The Society for the Protection of Ancient Buildings, 37 Spital Square, London E1 6DY (tel. 071 377 1644; fax 071 247 5296)

The Georgian Group, 37 Spital Square, London E1 6DY (tel. 071 377 1722; fax 071 247 3441)

The Victorian Society, 1 Priory Gardens, London W4 1TT (tel. 081 994 1019; fax 081 995 4895)

The Twentieth Century Society, 1 Priory Gardens, London W4 1TT (tel. 081 994 3201; fax 081 995 4895)

Inquiries about local amenity societies should in the first instance be made of The Civic Trust, 17 Carlton House Terrace, London SW1Y 5AW (tel. 071 930 0914; fax 071 321 0180). Inquiries should also be made of the local planning authority (where the initial contact should be with the Conservation Officer, if any).

Local History and Archaeological Societies

Contacts and addresses for local historical societies can be obtained from the British Association for Local History, Shopwyke Manor Barn, Chichester, West Sussex PO20 6BG (tel. 0243 787639; fax 0243 787636).

Contacts and addresses for local archaeological societies can be obtained from the Council for British Archaeology (see above).

Natural History

Arthur Rank Centre, Church and Conservation Project, National Agricultural Centre, Stoneleigh Park, Warwickshire CV8 2LZ (tel. 0203 696969; fax 0203 696900)

English Nature, Northminster House, Peterborough PE1 1UA (tel. 0733 340345; fax 0733 68834)

Yew Tree Campaign, c/o The Conservation Foundation, 1 Kensington Gore, London SW7 2AR (tel. 071 823 8842)

The name and address of the local wildlife trust can be obtained from the Royal Society for Nature Conservation, The Green, Witham Park, Waterside South, Lincoln LN5 7JR (tel. 0522 544400; fax 0522 511616).

More useful names and addresses will be found in *The Living Churchyard Information Pack*, available (price £6) from the Arthur Rank Centre, Church and Conservation Project (see above), and in *The Churchyards Handbook* (published by Church House Publishing).

Local Authority Associations

The Association of County Councils, Eaton House, 66a Eaton Square, London SW1W 9BH (tel. 071 235 1200; fax 071 235 8458)

The Association of District Councils, Chapter House, 26 Chapter Street, London SW1P 4ND (tel. 071 233 6848; fax 071 233 6551)

The Association of Metropolitan Authorities, 35 Great Smith Street, London SW1P 3BJ (tel. 071 222 8100; fax 071 222 0878)

APPENDIX H

FURTHER READING AND VIDEOS

Care of Churches, Churchyards and Contents – General

How to Look After Your Church (3rd ed. 1991); Church House Publishing

The Churchyards Handbook, by Peter Burman and the Very Revd Henry Stapleton (3rd ed. 1988); Church House Publishing

A Guide to Church Inspection and Repair (revised 1986); Church House Publishing

Looking After Your Church (video); Council for the Care of Churches

The Repair of Historic Buildings: Advice on Principles and Methods, by Christopher Brereton (1991); English Heritage (Building 12, Cherry Hill Estate, Old, Northants NN6 9QY – tel. 0604 781163)

English Heritage Policy Statement: New Work in Historic Churches; English Heritage

Department of the Environment Circular No. 8/87: Historic Buildings and Conservation Areas; Her Majesty's Stationery Office

Guide to the Parochial Registers and Records Measure 1978 (revised ed. 1992); Church House Publishing

The first three of the above books contain fuller lists for further reading, including complete lists of relevant publications by Church House Publishing and by the Council for the Care of Churches and lists of other books on specialised subjects.

History, Archaeology and Natural History

Recording a Church: An Illustrated Glossary, by Thomas Cocke, Donald Finlay, Richard Halsey and Elizabeth Williamson (2nd ed. 1984); Council for British Archaeology

The English Heritage Book of Church Archaeology, by Warwick Rodwell (1989); Batsford

Churches in the Landscape, by Richard Morris (1988); Dent

Department of the Environment Planning Policy Guidance Note 16: Archaeology and Planning; Her Majesty's Stationery Office

In Memoriam (video); English Heritage (Building 12, Cherry Hill Estate, Old, Northants NN6 9QY tel. 0604 781163)

Wildlife in the Churchyard – the Plants and Animals of God's Acre, by Francesa Greenoak (1993); Little Brown & Co.

Nature in Churchyards (leaflet) (4th ed. 1993); Arthur Rank Centre, Church and Conservation Project

The Living Churchyard Information Pack; Arthur Rank Centre, Church and Conservation Project

Discovering Churchyard Wildlife Survey (leaflet), by Marya Parker; Suffolk Wildlife Trust, Brooke House, The Green, Ashbocking, Suffolk IP6 9JY

Geology in the Churchyard (leaflet); The Geologists' Association, Burlington House, Piccadilly, London W1V 9AG

Bats in Churches, by Tony Mitchell-Jones; Council for the Care of Churches

How to Record Graveyards, by Jeremy Jones; Council for British Archaeology

Monuments and their Inscriptions: a Practical Guide, by H Leslie White; Society of Genealogists, 14 Charterhouse Buildings, Goswell Road, London EC1M 7BA

The Churchyards Handbook and *The Living Churchyard Information Pack* contain fuller lists for further reading.

Legal

The Faculty Jurisdiction of the Church of England: Care of Churches and Churchyards, by George Newsom (2nd ed. 1993), Sweet & Maxwell

The Law of the Parish Church, by Dale (6th ed. 1989); Butterworths

A Handbook for Churchwardens and Parochial Church Councillors, by Kenneth MacMorran, E Garth Moore and Timothy Briden (1989 ed.); Mowbray

For reference

The Canons of the Church of England (5th ed. 1993); Church House Publishing

The Opinions of the Legal Advisory Commission of the General Synod of the Church of England (6th ed. 1985 with supplements 1990 & 1991; new edition planned for 1993); Church House Publishing

Moore's Introduction to English Canon Law (3rd ed. 1992); Mowbray

Halsbury's Laws of England (4th ed.) Vol. 14, title Ecclesiastical Law; Butterworths

Halsbury's Statutes of England (4th ed.) Vol. 14, title Ecclesiastical Law; Butterworths

Listed Buildings and Conservation Areas, by Charles Mynors (1989); Longman

Listed Buildings, by Roger Suddards (2nd ed., 1988); Sweet & Maxwell

The Cambridge Guide to Historic Buildings Law (1988); Cambridge City Council (Shire Hall, Castle Hill, Cambridge CB1 0AP)

Wildlife and Countryside Act 1981; Her Majesty's Stationery Office